RECOVERED

Dedicated to all of those who walk around believing that they are not good enough. Those who are looking for truth that they actually had as a child, and still have, but have forgotten.

Published by Todd Sylvester Inspires, LLC.

Edited by Valleen Day
Design and Layout by Frank Day

> **Addiction is your wake up call to your greatness.**

TSylvtr

This information is not meant to be a replacement for medications or in-patient treatment centers.
Some conditions require immediate attention and should be handled through the appropriate groups and organizations.

If you need emergency services, call 911 or go to the nearest hospital emergency room.

To encourage people to seek out medical attention for an overdose or for follow-up care after naloxone has been administered, 40 states and the District of Columbia have enacted some form of a Good Samaritan or 911 drug immunity law. These laws generally provide immunity from arrest, charge or prosecution for certain controlled substance possession and paraphernalia offenses when a person who is either experiencing an opiate-related overdose or observing one calls 911 for assistance or seeks medical attention.

If you are thinking about harming yourself or attempting suicide, tell someone who can help right away.Emergencies - Please use the following resources:

NATIONAL SUICIDE PREVENTION LINE:
1-800-273-TALK

SUBSTANCE ABUSE AND MENTAL HEALTH SERVICES ADMINISTRATION (SAMHSA)
1-800-662-HELP

NATIONAL ALLIANCE ON MENTAL ILLNESS
WWW.NAMI.ORG

ABOUT TODD

Todd currently works as an Addictive Voice Recognition Counselor at a reputable treatment center for those struggling with drug or alcohol addiction, where he provides one-on-one mentoring to both local and international clients. He also serves as a Mentor & Personal-Development Coach for those looking to get more out of life. Along with addiction recovery support, he has a variety of outreach programs which fall under the umbrella of his foundational business, Todd Sylvester Inspires (TSI).

In 1989 he founded the non-profit, anti-drug entity Sly Dog "Drug Free That's Me," which features a sought-after education program for elementary schools. This program has encouraged over 100,000 school-age students, emphasizing principles of positive self- talk, personal commitment, goal setting, and character building.

Todd spent his youth addicted to drugs and alcohol. Through his own recovery and newfound awareness, Todd learned that more powerful than any addiction was the power of the human soul. Over the past 25 years Todd has discovered and taught universal principles that have empowered thousands to conquer addiction, crush compulsive behaviors, and change their limiting belief systems.

Todd's story was recently told through a popular YouTube clip that received over 1 million views and has been translated into 3 languages. Todd has conducted over 1,000 speaking engagements and close to 15,000 individual coaching sessions.

WHY I DO THIS

Not long ago I sat down with David Mead, who is the partner of British-American author, motivational speaker, and organisational consultant, Simon Sinek, to compose my why statement.

Standing shoulder to shoulder with Simon Sinek and the "Start With Why" team, David is globally recognized as the HOW guy to Simon's WHY. Using his years of practical experience, David co-authored *Find Your Why* with Simon Sinek and Peter Docker.

I did this to fully realize my focus and passion. It is what lead me to writing all of the content I cover with my clients and am about to share with you. It is how I deliver motivational speeches all over the country, to students and prisoners alike.

Here is my why:

"To ignite the imagination to the reality that there is nothing wrong with you, so that you can ignite the same in others"

To break that down—There is nothing wrong with you! By the end of this program, I hope you believe me so you can move forward with your head high, then pass it on to someone else.

> **We don't rise to the level of our expectations, we fall to the level of our training.**
>
> - U.S. Military

AN
UNCOMMON
WAY OF THINKING

I had a client that, on his first day in one of my psycho-educational groups, learned something so powerful. Yet, it's something I think we all take for granted.

I asked this client why he was there? He responded, "I can't stop doing drugs." I said, "Did you do drugs today?"

He said, "No."

I continued, "Did you do drugs yesterday?"

He said, "no."

I again asked, "Did you do drugs the day before that?"

He responded, "No I did not."

I then said, "How did you do that?"

He looked a bit confused by my challenge questioning. I waited for a response.

He finally said, "I just chose not to?" I could tell he was not sure if it was the right answer.

I said, "See, stop lying to yourself. Here you are clean right now and you're telling yourself a lie that you can't stop."

You could see the truth hit him like a slap in the face. In that moment, he learned that he is in control of his own sobriety and that the only thing that had been stopping him from getting clean up until that point was his way of thinking. Once he realized the power of his thoughts and acknowledged his capability of being clean, he began thinking he could be clean and he acted like he was.

I share this with you now so that you can use this reference as you go through the rest of the guide, in hopes that it inspires you and keeps you believing that you have the power to choose to be clean.

INTRO

I'd like to welcome you to recoverED, my specialized program to help you with a new way to view addiction and recovery.

Recently, I sat in a room across from a woman who had been working very hard to overcome her addictions. This woman was my client and at this moment, she was experiencing a breakthrough.

While this breakthrough was wonderful to witness, it wasn't difficult to recognize. For the past 25 years, I had devoted my life to helping others overcome addictions. I'd worked as a speaker, a life- coach, and a clinician. Throughout these years, I had provided countless people with knowledge and tools they could utilize to overcome their addictions. I had witnessed many breakthroughs.

I had watched people reclaim their lives from addiction.

A breakthrough is a life-changing moment, filled with an almost immeasurable sense of power and possibility. And yet... it often arrives with a sense of calm and clarity. Because a breakthrough is the discovery of truth. Often, it's the rediscovery of a truth that has merely been forgotten.

Stephanie's breakthrough didn't arrive with any new information. I had simply reminded her of three basic truths that she had always known but – as a result of a lifetime of drug, alcohol, and self- sabotage – had disregarded along the way.

Stephanie left our session inspired by her awareness and newfound motivation to achieve true sobriety. Filled with hope, she shared her experience with a group director at another treatment center... and was promptly scolded. Stephanie's breakthrough did not fit with this program director's view of the world. He refused to accept it and backed that refusal with a Master's Degree in addiction.

Stephanie returned to me, crushed and confused. She had not even had the opportunity to put her hope into action before an attempt had been made to stomp it out.

I understood Stephanie's pain and sense of helplessness. The truth of my life is that I had spent a great deal of my youth addicted to drugs and alcohol. During this dark period, I disregarded many of the things that were most important to me. I have lived through sadness, self-hatred, and a very real plan to end my own life.

I don't have a Master's Degree or a Ph.D. I am not classically trained in addiction recovery. But for the past quarter of a century, I have lived a life that is free from drugs and alcohol. I am not a recovering addict. I am recoverED! And I have helped others do the same.

Through my experience with both addiction and sobriety, I have discovered truths that, if understood, are the keys to unlocking sobriety, releasing anxiety, and developing a deep, healthy love of one's self.

A NEW
DEFINITION
OF SOBRIETY

Every rehabilitation program and coach you encounter will likely have different experience with getting clean. They will also have different philosophies for treatment, different terms for similar experiences, feelings, or references. One thing that really sets my program apart from others is how I use the term "sobriety." To a lot of people, sobriety means drug free but I believe that it is actually the periods between using. The ultimate goal in an addiction recovery journey is to say you are clean! Clean means, I am done.

LOVE = SACRIFICE

If you love someone you will sacrifice for them and it's no different than if you love you. You'll sacrifice for you if you really love you! One of the questions I ask my clients is, "Would you ever give heroin or alcohol to your child, niece, or nephew?" Their answer is usually something like, "Never in a million years!" When I ask why? The answer is, "Because that is just wrong." I will then say, "Because you _____(blank) them?" Their response, "Because I LOVE them."

And if you love you, which you should learn how to do through this program, you will sacrifice for you. Whether that means you wake up early and workout or if you say no to the drug that someone offers you.

Love of Self will prove to be the most powerful antidote over any unwanted or addictive behaviors – PERIOD!

SOBER

I'm an addict

Always in Recovery

The period in between using

Counting Days

White Knuckling

VS

CLEAN

It's Over

Empowered

RecoverED

I'm Clean

Relaxed

No need to count if I am done

Freedom

THINGS THAT
WILL NOT FLY

Before you start this program, there are a few things that will not fly. If you want to be successful you are going to have to unlearn a belief system that our culture has cultivated in you since you were born.

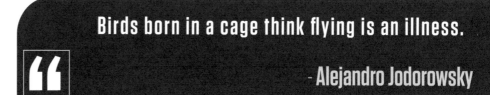

Birds born in a cage think flying is an illness.

- Alejandro Jodorowsky

Just like you, a bird is born to be free. Metaphorically, living within the cage like a trapped bird doesn't let you have a wider perspective of what you can experience in life. There are people who settle for what they have heard and believe that's just the way it is. Labels are cages. When you speak or think something you manifest it. It becomes your reality. When we label ourselves with things like the list below, they become our own self-made cages, and thus will not fly from now on.

- I will always be an addict
- I am powerless
- I have a disease
- I am broken
- I can't do this
- Something is wrong with me
- It's just who I am

- It's too hard
- I was triggered
- I will always be like this
- I can't do it
- Life is too hard
- I'm not good enough
- My problems are too big - it's impossible to overcome

THE WORST
BULLY
YOU WILL EVER ENCOUNTER

Here is the truth about how dangerous negative self-talk can be. We all have days when negative thoughts get us down, but when negative thinking becomes habitual it can be devastating.

Have you ever heard a voice in your head that says:

◆ "I'm not good enough"
◆ "I'm not strong enough"
◆ "I can't do it"

We've all felt the effects of negative self-talk. Sometimes life's circumstances feel so adverse that we think there must be something wrong with us. "Why can't I live the life I want to? Why can't I just be happy?" We all have days when negative thoughts get us down, but when negative thinking becomes habitual it can be devastating.

Just like a drug addiction, self-destructive thoughts usually start out small. We beat ourselves up for small mistakes we make throughout the day. We tell ourselves negative things like: "That was stupid, why can't I get this right?" "Why do I even bother?"

If our bad feelings go unchecked, we might move on to graver assaults on our self-image: "I'll never be good enough," "Nobody likes me," "I'm totally worthless."

From there, things have the potential to take a sharp turn for the worse. Next thing we know, we have thoughts like, "I don't deserve to live," "I'd be better off dead."
That's what happened to me.

During the years of my addiction, I learned a whole new meaning of the word misery. I won't lie to you, at first, drugs made me happy. Being high felt incredible. I was always the cool guy at the party. I was popular and people loved me.
But it didn't last. My highs quickly became lows, and I didn't know why. I wanted to quit, but I felt powerless to do so. It's like there was a voice inside my head telling me how pathetic I was, how damaged and worthless.

Eventually I got to the point where I couldn't take it anymore. The voice in my head had torn me down to my bare bones. There was nothing left. And so I decided to end my life.

Looking back at that time, I realize how irrational the idea was. I had been alive for 22 years, and the time and the actual time I wanted to kill myself spanned only 3 short days. But it was real. I really was going to do it.
How did it get so bad? Why did I beat myself up to the point where I thought I deserved to die? What was this voice in my head?

I've come to call this voice The Bully.

WHAT IS THE BULLY?

Think back to a time when you felt anxiety, or depression. Think of a time when you were trying to change a negative behavior but felt powerless to do so.

When I was young I thought that I was the only one who heard a negative voice in my head, but over the years of coaching others, I've discovered that EVERYONE does. Everyone has a Bully.

The Bully embodies every negative thought we have about ourselves. It's the voice that resides in every one of us and tries to keep us from loving ourselves and experiencing joy.

I can guarantee that you have heard the voice of The Bully in your own life. Think back to a time when you felt anxiety, or depression. Think of a time when you were trying to change a negative behavior but felt powerless to do so.

What were your thoughts? What kinds of things did you believe about yourself?

That's the voice of The Bully.

The Bully tells us that we have no choice, that we are powerless to change and will always be the way we are, that we are a victim of our circumstances, that we are broken, damaged, and less-than.

The Bully reinforces these negative thoughts until they become our beliefs. And that's where The Bully becomes truly dangerous because our belief systems shape who we are.

Our beliefs define us, drive us, and guide us to make choices about how we will live our lives. If we give The Bully the power to change our beliefs, there's no telling what awful lives of self-destruction we might lead.

I know you've heard this voice before and I know it has caused pain and heartache in your life. But I also know that you don't have to let him rule your life. You can stand up to The Bully and change your beliefs about yourself.

The first step in beating The Bully is learning to recognize its voice.

THE BULLY ALWAYS LIES

There's one thing that all of The Bully's attacks have in common. They are all utterly and invariably FALSE.

Everything The Bully tells you is untrue!

I know it might feel at the time that what The Bully tells you is the truth, but that's exactly The Bully's intention! The Bully tells you lies about yourself and then expects you to believe them. And The Bully won't hold up until you believe the garbage it spews.

But you don't HAVE to. You can confidently know that when The Bully tries to get you down, whatever it's saying is untrue.

When The Bully says that something is "too hard for you," that's a lie. Sure, a certain experience or event might be hard, but it's not too hard. When you really think about it, there's nothing you can't handle. You will survive.

When The Bully says you're powerless to change, that's a lie as well! You have the ability to choose what you want to be and how you want to live, even though it doesn't feel like it sometimes.

During my addiction I believed everything The Bully told me. The Bully dished it out and I took it—no questions asked. It took a change in my Belief System to realize that The Bully was lying to me. I wasn't worthless; I was valuable! I wasn't helpless; I was powerful!

The only reason I WAS miserable, depressed, and addicted is because I BELIEVED what The Bully was telling me. As soon as I realized that The Bully was lying to me, my life started changing. It was as simple as that. I can guarantee that for everything The Bully says about you, the opposite is true. I know it's difficult to believe at first, but it's the truth.

Just try it. Every time The Bully says something negative to you, say the opposite to yourself instead. If The Bully says "No one likes you," say out loud, "Everyone loves me!" When The Bully says "You're not good enough," say instead "I'm everything I want to be!"

As you come to realize that The Bully lies, you will have more power to take a stand. You know that what The Bully say is not true. Deep down you know it.

It takes strength to withstand The Bully's attacks at first, but over time it will become easier. The truth about who you really are will become a part of your Belief System and your life will change.

THE BULLY IS POWERLESS

The second thing you need to know is that The Bully is completely powerless. The Bully can't make you do, think, or believe anything you don't want to.

At times it seems like The Bully never shuts up, like it's the one who's making you feel the way you do, and like there's nothing you can do to stop it— but that's not the case.

The truth is, you are the only one who can make choices for yourself. No one else in the world can make you feel anything you don't want to—especially not The Bully.

When we take the lies of The Bully and make them a part of our reality, it's because we are CHOOSING to believe what it says. We are choosing to succumb to The Bully's attacks.

But if you can choose to listen to The Bully and make its put-downs a part of your belief system, you can also choose to ignore its voice. You have the power to say NO, to refuse to listen to The Bully and replace its hurtful words with the truth.

I'm not saying that The Bully's attacks will stop. I have now been clean and sober for 26 years and The Bully still comes to visit every now and then. But now I know how to deal with it. I know that The Bully is a liar and has no power over me.

The Bully can whisper. The Bully can scream. But The Bully can't force us to do a single thing. You are the only person with power over what you choose to do and feel.

THE TRUTH IS THE CURE

You may be thinking at this point: "Great. The Bully can't make me do anything I don't choose to, but it's never going to stop trying? How am I supposed to deal with its perpetual abuse?"

There is one way to silence the voice of The Bully, and that's with the truth.

When we tell ourselves the truth about who we are, we start thinking differently and we begin to shape our belief systems for the better. When we believe that we are powerful, capable, and creative, we become so. When we speak the truth, it give us the power change our reality.

The thing about The Bully is ... The Bully can't handle the truth. It's the part of yourself that knows only lies and negativity. When you constantly speak the truth, The Bully's voice will become drowned out. Eventually, you will come to the point where you can hardly hear the voice of The Bully at all.

Remember, The Bully is just that—a bully! You can stand up to it. You can beat it. You can make your life YOUR LIFE again.

PRINCIPLES

(THE INWARD HEAVEN)

Like anything else in life, creating a true love of one's self requires practice. It can't happen simply by reading this and won't come merely by attending a seminar or spending time at a rehabilitation center. A fundamental shift in mindset is necessary, as is a willingness to embrace a new set of beliefs and use those beliefs as a guide for life.

I discovered three beliefs through my own recovery and I have watched these beliefs change countless lives. I want you learn them. I want you to be intimate with them. I want you to believe them at the center of who you are – at your core.

With these positive, affirming beliefs, you can achieve love of self. Read these to yourself often. Memorize them and say them aloud:

- ◆ I HAVE THE DIGNITY TO CHOOSE
- ◆ I AM A MASTERFUL CREATOR
- ◆ I AM POWERFUL BEYOND MEASURE

If these ideas seem foreign to you, it might be because they are in direct contrast to belief systems people commonly carry. Let's explore, in greater depth, each of these three founding principles.

I HAVE THE DIGNITY TO CHOOSE

The foundation of any change is the belief that you have the ability to choose. You can change your situation and your circumstances. No matter what state your life is in, you can choose right now, in this very moment, to make it different.

The pull of addiction is very powerful. At least… it can feel that way. Our old ways always pull us in and make us believe that our future is already determined by choices we have made in the past. The truth is that you always have the power and ability to choose, no matter what the circumstances. And this realization is, in itself, a fundamentally empowering truth.

You can choose to be clean and sober today. You can choose to fight back against the voice of The Bully. But remember that what you resist persists. Choose to set yourself apart from The Bully and when you hear his voice… laugh at him!

Consider the words of George Bernard Shaw:

> People are always blaming their circumstances for what they are. I don't believe in circumstances. The people who get on in this world are the people who get up and look for the circumstances they want, and if they can't find them, make them.

I AM A MASTERFUL CREATOR

When we exercise our power and ability to choose, in that moment, we become CREATORS.

When we choose to turn off the TV and engage our minds by reading something positive, we are CREATING feelings of positivity and joy in our lives. When we choose to listen to a small idea like "pull over and give this girl at the lemonade stand all of your change," we are creating feelings of abundance, caring, and happiness.

Everything in our lives – good and bad – was created by US. The law of attraction states that "like attracts like," which means that every time we make a conscious choice, we are ATTRACTING that reality to us. Our mind is a garden. Our thoughts, feelings, and choices are seeds that we plant in that garden. These seeds grow, in our minds, into fully-grown belief systems.

Will we plant an organized, beautiful, and intentional garden? Or will our minds become overrun by weeds and chaos? The choice is ours.

You must learn to separate yourself from the voice of The Bully. When The Bully arrives to declare that you are a powerless victim, you must be able to say to yourself: I am a masterful creator.
Most importantly... you must believe it.

I AM POWERFUL BEYOND MEASURE

When we make positive choices, and we begin to see creations that grow from those choices, we soon see that we are POWERFUL.

As a culture (and especially as "addicts"), we are taught that we are weak and powerless. But when we learn to see the small evidences in our lives, we also learn that we are more powerful than we can even comprehend.

YOU have the power over your own life. You, and you alone, have the power to create the world around you. You can choose to go at the world alone or you can choose to bring good friends into your life and find a connection with a higher power. You don't have to wait for anyone to rescue you - your inner being holds the power to create anything you want and need.

When you CHOOSE to not listen to The Bully, you CREATE thoughts, feelings, and circumstances that make you POWERFUL.

You are more powerful than your problems. You are more powerful than your addictions!

WHO AM I?

Think of someone you consider to be a good person. If that person sat down in front of you, what characteristics does this person possess? How would you describe them? (Some examples might be: Honest, hardworking, loving, compassionate, kind, etc.)

_____

_____

_____

_____

_____

Now, take a look at that list—You just described yourself!

The things you see within others exist within ourselves.

This is one of the most challenging lessons we have to learn. Every person we meet in life is showing up at the perfect time in our lives to reflect something we need to heal within ourselves. The people with whom you interact are showing you who you are and ultimately providing you with an opportunity to love yourself.

Now think about this—How long should a baby take to learn to walk? Until the baby is _____ months/years old. The right answer is until. It will not learn to walk until it learns to walk.

Imagine watching a baby learn to walk. What characteristics are demonstrated? (Some examples are: Determined, resilient, confident, forgiving, believing, etc.)

_____

_____

_____

_____

Where do you think they get those characteristics? The answer is—they were born with them. They came from God and are a part of their DNA.

What does that mean about you?

This is also YOU! You have the exact same characteristics and abilities you were born with, they are ingrained in you, and you can learn to walk again.

LIFE-CHANGING BELIEFS

When King Louis XVI was dethroned and decapitated during the French Revolution, his son Louis XVII, the "Lost Dauphin," was taken captive by conspirators against the throne. According to legend, his captors believed that if they could break the prince morally, they could void any claim he had to the throne and destroy the monarchy forever.

They exposed him to every vice they could muster: alcohol, fattening foods, foul language, and lustful women. They tried incessantly to force the prince to participate in these vices, but he never did. He never caved under pressure. He never once compromised his morals.

When his captors asked him why he never indulged, he simply replied:

> "I CANNOT DO WHAT YOU ASK, FOR I WAS BORN TO BE A KING."

The boy knew who he was and did not compromise on that, even in the face of temptation and adversity. You can do the exact same thing.

Watch the Video, "Answering the deep question of Existence" - Neale Donald Walsch. You can find it on YouTube by searching or typing this URL: (https://www.youtube.com/watch?reload=9&v=QgRgZ7-1pZO)

So, who are you? Your answer should be something like, you are not separate from God.

What are the characteristics of God or your Higher Power? (Some examples are: Loving, kind, compassionate, confident, honest, etc.)

_____

_____

_____

_____

_____

Just like the previous examples, this should illustrate for you that you have amazing qualities within you. Qualities that come from a higher power, as part of your DNA, like a gift at birth.

⬦ Assignment

Read Awe Therapy (Page 22) 3 times

Now take a minute to reflect and write down the answer to this question: Who are you?

Describe who you are in detail:

_____

_____

_____

_____

_____

_____

_____

_____

_____

_____

_____

_____

_____

_____

_____

Whenever you feel like you are losing sight of who you are, come back to this assignment and repeat it.

WHO ARE YOU?

You are an awe inspiring individual and when Jason Silva says, "Cracked open with Awe," that's what you do for me and for the world. We are a sum total of all our beliefs, good and bad. It's based on the story we tell ourselves about ourselves, which on paper isn't always true. We are not our jobs, cars, homes, bank accounts, we are not even our spouses, kids, or friends. We are not addicts, alcoholics, we are not anxious, worriers, sad, or depressed.

Eckhart Tolle says, "You are the universe expressing itself as a human for a little while." You are inexplicable beauty, love, light, truth, and joy. Joy is our natural state and we experience this when we live in the present moment - now. The past is gone forever and the future hasn't happened yet, so all we have is now and when we live in the now, the Universe answers with pinpoint precision and a manifestation of our completeness.

Carl Sagan says, "We are made of star stuff. Every one of us is, in the cosmic perspective, precious. If a human disagrees with you, let him live. In a hundred billion galaxies, you will not find another."

You are magnificent! Gunilla Norris said, "Within each of us, there is a silence, a silence as vast as the Universe. And when we experience that silence, we remember who we are." You are greatness in motion. When you pinpoint your attention on this mathematical fact, you discover what you already knew as a child. Greatness is not some rare DNA strand that only a few us possess. It's not an illusion or some mystical concept that eludes us at every turn. It flourishes in your awareness of who you really are. Some people say they were born with it, others tell themselves.

Check out this quote:

> *"There are no ordinary people. You have never talked to a mere mortal. Nations, cultures, arts, civilizations - these are mortal, and their life is to ours as the life of a gnat. But it is immortals whom we joke with, work with, marry, snub and exploit...*
>
> *It is a serious thing to live in a society of possible gods and goddesses, to remember that the dullest most uninteresting person you can talk to may one day be a creature which, if you saw it now, you would be strongly tempted to worship...*
>
> *It is in the light of these overwhelming possibilities, it is with the awe and the circumspection proper to them, that we should conduct all of our dealings with one another, all friendships, all loves, all play, all politics. There are no ordinary people."*

> - C.S. Lewis, The Weight of Glory

RESHAPING YOUR
SELF-IMAGE

🔍 Overview

I have already introduced you to the bully but now we are going to talk about how you can use that knowledge and apply to reshape your self-image.

Everyone has a battle with a negative voice inside their minds. Some worse than others but we all have it.

FROM STUPID TO BRILLIANT

I had a client who had this belief that he was stupid. It was revealed to me because of his responses in The Bully Playlist assignment, which you will also complete at the end of this section. At the top of his list, the number one thing he said to himself because of the negative voice in his head was, "I am stupid." It became a part of his belief system because he had said it so much. I asked him when that had started and he said that when he was in 5th grade at parent-teacher conference, he overheard his teacher tell his parents, "Your son is not very bright." He overhears this and believes in that moment that he was stupid. He started telling himself that over and over to the point that he started to believe. He then went on to prove it by getting bad grades, hating school, and eventually dropping. Sitting across from me now, 45 years later, I ask him, "How has this held you back in life?" He said, "I didn't go to college because I didn't think I was smart enough. I take low paying jobs because I don't think I can do any better. I walk with my head down and won't look anyone in the eye. I isolate myself a lot. I won't read a book out loud in front of someone. I am just miserable." I said to him, "Well, that is one reason you slam heroin." He asked me what I meant and I explained that belief dictates our behavior. He believed he was stupid so his behavior mirrored that. I went on to tell him that he had to start believing the truth and the truth is that he actually is brilliant. I told him every time from that point on when that negative thought came to his mind, I wanted him to label that thought as "it," or the bully, and tell himself the opposite. So for example, "I Todd am brilliant." I had him practice it in front of me and he almost threw up when he said it, he wasn't used to telling himself something like that and he didn't believe it. The truth was, he really was brilliant. He went on to tell himself this over and over again until he finally started to feel comfortable and believe it.

To get to that point, I challenged him to say it in the mirror at least 400 times every day for a week, which was 2800 times. I had him tally it and write a journal entry at the end of each day. He completed the challenge faithfully and it was remarkable to see that he changed his belief system from it. He will now look you in the eye, read a book out loud, won't isolate, and hasn't slammed heroin in over 4 years. It sounds really simplistic but that is the power of belief. The way a belief system is formed is by a sustained thought—taking the old belief, making it positive or different, and reinforcing it with repetition.

Knowing the truth about who we are can make an enormous difference in how we live our lives and how we respond to the put-downs of our own personal Bully—the part of our minds that produces negative self-talk. If we really know how capable and powerful we are, there's nothing The Bully can say that will derail us. We will never falter.

As it stands, The Bully preys upon our insecurities and tells us lies about ourselves to try and get us to engage in negative behaviors. Just like in the story of the young prince, The Bully is relentless.

While The Bully has many lies, and the specific language The Bully uses may vary from person to person, all of your negative self-talk tends to center on three negative beliefs:

1. I am powerless to change, and will always be the way I am.

2. I am a victim of my circumstances.

3. I am broken and "less than."

Besides being untrue, each of these negative beliefs tap into the core of what makes people miserable. Sadly, these are beliefs that people often have about themselves. All negative beliefs are founded in helplessness, hopelessness, and an unwillingness to change.

Listening to the lies of The Bully leads to a destructive lifestyle of addiction and self-hatred. If we buy into it enough, those lies can become our beliefs.

Many reading this may have made the Bully's lies a part of their belief system—but I have good news: you can change your beliefs!

Remember the 3 Foundational Beliefs that you learned earlier— you can use these to counter the lies of The Bully:

1. I have the dignity and ability to choose.

2. I am a masterful creator.

3. I am powerful beyond measure.

These are the beliefs that helped me make breakthroughs in my own addiction recovery. We are not victims.

I know that's often the stance people take when confronting their problems, but ultimately this attitude leads to despondency and inaction. In fact, the opposite is true: we have the opportunity to choose at every turn in life.

Learning that you have the ability to choose is one of the most important steps in recovering from addictions and learning to love yourself. By recognizing this truth, you liberate yourself from the paralyzing grasp of The Bully. You can no longer hide behind the excuse of not being able to do anything about your situation ... because you can!

No matter what position you find yourself in, no matter how bad you think your problems are or how deeply addicted you have become, you have the power to turn your life around and choose something else. You can choose a better life!

> " People are always blaming their circumstances for what they are. I don't believe in circumstances. The people who get on in this world are the people who get up and look for the circumstances they want, and if they can't find them, make them.
>
> - George Bernard Shaw

Now I recognize that you don't choose your circumstances in the sense that you can't always control what things happen to you in life—but that doesn't make you a victim! You CAN choose how you handle your circumstances and how you will allow them to make you feel.

Typically we consider circumstances to be the one thing have no power over, but in reality, they're all we have. In any given moment we are given the gift of our present conditions. If we choose to embrace them, learn from them, and enjoy them, we can become the master of our circumstances.

The Bully will try to convince you that you have no choice, that you are stuck or hopeless. Don't believe him. Remember, choice isn't just something you're capable of, it's something you're worthy of. You deserve to choose the life you like. You deserve Love of Self. When you recognize your ability to choose and start making choices that will better your life, you become a creator.

Every person has the faculty to create, but not everyone uses it. When we allow ourselves to be shaped and manipulated by powers outside of ourselves, we are denying our god-given potential to create.

By instead choosing the life we want, we are in turn creating it. If we choose not to feel grief over a mistake or hardship we are creating feelings of joy and peace in our lives. If we choose not to let someone's flaws make us angry or irritated, we create love. If we choose that we want a life of prosperity, we will create wealth, good health, and joy!
The truth is, you can create ANYTHING you want in life. Anything your heart desires, anything that is good and positive, you have the power to create! You can bring it into existence, make it a part of your identity, and allow it to enrich your life. We often think of creation as a trait that only gods and artists possess. But when you think about it, what does an artist actually do? An artist envisions in his mind something that inspires him, something that he wishes to create, and then he brings that something from thought to reality.

That's all that creation is! Taking our thoughts and making them our reality. And every single one of us is capable of doing that. This is where choice comes in. If we choose to believe that we are broken, damaged, and have no hope of recovery, THAT is the reality we will create.

On the other hand, if we choose to believe that we are capable, powerful, and full of love, we will be able to overcome ANY negative behavior. We will be able to beat back The Bully and choose the life we want to live.I am powerful beyond measure

This is the Foundational Belief that people tend to struggle with the most.

Sadly, so many people believe that they are powerless. It is HIGHLY prevalent in the culture of addicts. The thought that they might be "powerful beyond measure" is ludicrous to them. They can't even imagine it in their wildest dreams.

One such person was my client, Travis. When I met Travis he was addicted to hard drugs and had been thrown in jail for possession of heroin. He wanted to turn his life around, but he felt powerless to do so.

When I first told him he was powerful beyond measure, he laughed in my face, but eventually he agreed to give the belief a try. I challenged him to recite the phrase, "I, Travis, am powerful beyond measure" 400 times each day.

At first Travis struggled. He said the words but they were empty. He didn't really believe them. After several days however, he discovered his true power. He was able to recite the words and truly feel them coursing through him.

By the end of my time working with Travis, he told me that he positively knew that he was powerful beyond measure and that he exercised that power every day. As you begin to create the world around you, you will quickly recognize your own power. You will discover that there's nothing you can't do!

Now when I say power, I'm not talking about magic and unicorns. I'm talking about the power of thought.

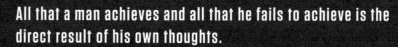

All that a man achieves and all that he fails to achieve is the direct result of his own thoughts.

- James Allen

Thought shapes our reality! Thought is our reality. We always have power over our own thoughts, feelings, and intentions, and therefore, we have power over every aspect of our reality. We can create anything! We are all-powerful.

In some cases, we will create literal tangible things, such as wealth or artwork. In other cases, we will merely use our power to change our perception of our world. Either way the result is the same! If you make the truth that you are powerful beyond measure a part of your belief system, your life will be filled with joy and Love of Self.

 Assignment

You have already read The Biggest Bully You'll Ever Encounter and learned about The Bully, now go watch the Bully video on my website: http://toddsylvesterinspires.com

Next, complete The Bully Playlist. What is your bully playlist? Write down any negative thoughts or limiting beliefs you have about yourself, that you face each day. Example: "I am stupid."

Then complete The Champion Playlist. Take each negative statement from your Bully Playlist and write the opposite and add your name to it. Example: i.e. "I, Alayna, am Brilliant."

MY BULLY PLAYLIST

_____   _____

_____   _____

_____   _____

_____   _____

_____   _____

_____   _____

_____   _____

_____   _____

_____   _____

MY CHAMPION PLAYLIST

_____   _____

_____   _____

_____   _____

_____   _____

_____   _____

_____   _____

_____   _____

_____   _____

Definition

ANXIETY: A misuse of your imagination.

Overview

I want to focus on the Power of Thoughts. Your thoughts create the emotion every time you have them. Guilt, shame, sadness, depression, fear, worry, anxiety, etc., all start with a thought. What do most of those examples have in common? They are pretty negative, right? Well, the same goes for the opposite of these. Love, expansion of your light, happiness, joy, excitement, etc., all start with a thought.

Anxiety is an emotion that most people are familiar with. They know what anxiety is, whether we have experienced it ourselves or have friends and family who have to work through it. Generally, anxiety comes from worrying about the future—or things that have not happened yet. It is a misuse of your imagination. The brain doesn't know the difference between a real event or if you imagine it.

The dictionary defines anxiety as A feeling of worry, nervousness, or unease, typically about an imminent event or something with an uncertain outcome. Anxiety is actually just a misuse of your imagination.

Think about the last time you watched a scary movie. Did you jump when something terrifying happened? Did you feel fear the same way the main characters did? I am willing to bet that you did because even though you know you walked into the movie with an understanding that whatever you see on the screen isn't real, the brains still believes it's real in the moment. With that in mind, you can see how being in control of your thoughts can really help you manage your emotions.

Time is something that we all get tripped up on every once in a while, whether it is the past or the future. Here is a break-down of both to help you understand why worrying about either will get you nowhere but stuck in negative emotions.

THE PAST

The Past is gone forever. You never get it back, you never have to go back to it, and it can never hurt you again. It is gone. When you think of your past and you beat yourself up for missed opportunities or for mistakes you have made, what emotions does this create inside of you? Guilt, shame, frustration, depression, sadness. All negative emotions. (Note: There is a difference, however, about thinking back on positive past experiences which make you feel good emotion.)

THE FUTURE

The Future hasn't happened hasn't happened yet. You have no idea what will happen or how anything will play out. When you think of your future and you catastrophize it, you think something bad is going to happen, I call it "future tripping." What emotions does this create inside of you? Fear, worry, anxiety. All emotions that will not serve you in the moment you should be living in. You can absolutely work toward the future and have goals without building anxious feelings around it with worry.

NOW

The now is really all we have. It is the only thing that you actually have control of. It means that you are not future tripping and you are not dwelling about the past. The past is gone forever and the future has not happened yet, so the truth is all we have is NOW – every second, it's now.

Think about some of the best times in your life. What was the emotion that you felt? Was it happiness and joy? Joy is our natural state. It is how we are meant to feel all the time. The problem is that we get stuck, often worrying about past or future, and we don't enjoy the now.

Let's go back to Elementary school when you were out on the playground for recess. What did you play? Tether ball? Four square? Really imagine it. Imagine a little you. Are you happy? I guarantee that you are because you didn't have to try. You were just being, being happy. This is because you are not in the past or the future.

That is the power of when we were a child. We loved ourselves, everyone, and everything. We had faith as big as the universe. We are in the now if we feel joy. If you ever need to feel joy and are stuck, think back to this example and try to focus on your now and the joy in it.

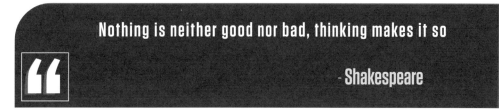
Nothing is neither good nor bad, thinking makes it so

- Shakespeare

I was working with a group in a recovery center. One of my clients came in late and I asked him where he had been. He responded with, "Oh, I am sorry. I was outside watching an ant pile and lost track of time." I thought to myself, "Well, this should be good." So he sits down and I tell him we are going to stop what we are doing while he tells us his experience with the ant pile. He was hesitant at first but then started telling us. He explained that he started watching it and lost track of time, like he had previously said but added that it was an amazing experience. I asked him to give us the details. So he said, "Well, I was watching these ants pick up a grain of sand and move it around. Digging up some dirt, going in and out of the holes. I could see their legs and antennas. Then I stepped back and watched how they worked, like a well oiled machine and it was one of the most incredible things I have ever seen." So I said to him, "Were you suffering?" He said, "Absolutely not!" I asked when the last time that happened to him. He said it was probably when he was a little kid. I said, "That's why you are here. How to figure out how to stop the suffering and experience joy again. Do you know what enlightenment is?"

My favorite definition is by Buddha, Enlightenment is the end of suffering. Enlightenment is also another word for joy, which is our natural state.

This client, when he experienced the ant pile, he was 9 days sober after 30 years of drinking. After losing his wife, his job, the respect of his children. But for that 40 minutes he was watching this ant pile, his suffering had ended. He was experience joy and enlightenment.

The moment one gives close attention to anything, even a blade of grass it becomes a mysterious, awesome, indescribably magnificent world in itself.

- Henry Miller

Tool

As you go through each day, try to recognize when you are future tripping or dwelling on the past. Remember that you can refocus on the now to feel joy and eliminate depression and anxiety.

Repeat this to yourself in those moments:

"All I have is now and my natural state is joy!"

Say it as if it is a truth (like an affirmation) and imagine yourself in your natural state.

" Enlightenment = The end of suffering.

- Buddha

BELIEF SYSTEMS

Roger Gilbert Bannister was a British middle-distance athlete and neurologist who ran the first 4-minute mile. At the 1952 Olympics in Helsinki, Bannister set a British record in the 1500 metres and finished in fourth place. This achievement strengthened his resolve to become the first athlete to finish the mile run in under four minutes.

He accomplished that feat on May 6, 1954 at Iffley Road track in Oxford, with Chris Chataway and Chris Brasher providing the pacing. When the announcer declared "The time was three...", the cheers of the crowd drowned out Bannister's exact time, which was 3 minutes and 59.4 seconds. He had attained this record with minimal training, while practicing as a junior doctor. Up until this point, the world believed that it was impossible to run a mile in that little amount of time.

Unfortunately, Bannister's record lasted just 46 days. However, people's belief system changed that day, including Roger's. Despite holding the title for a short period of time, he lead thousands of others to believe that they could do the same which was previously thought to be impossible. Since that time, over 20,000 people have done it. Belief dictates behavior, believe you can achieve more and you will.

> **Upon this little word belief hangs all our sorrows and joys.**
>
> **- James Allen**

If you were to randomly ask people on the street what they think about drug addicts and alcoholics, what do you think they would say?

Liars Cheaters No Good
Losers Criminals Weak
Sick Diseased

Chances are slim to none for success.

This type of cultural mentality around addictions forms beliefs about who people think they are. Also, we need talk about Roger Banister's story.

Belief systems are the stories we tell ourselves to define our personal sense of "reality." Every human being has a belief system that they utilize, and it is through this mechanism that we individually, "make sense" of the world around us. A belief is just a thought we continue to think over and over. Repetition deepens the impression or in other words creates a belief system, positive or negative.

"All behaviors are sponsored by beliefs. You cannot make a long-term change in behaviors without addressing the beliefs that underlie them. Seek to change beliefs, not behavior. After a belief, the behavior will change by itself. You can take whatever action you want to take to alter someone else's behavior or to stop it, but unless you alter the beliefs that produce such behavior, you will alter nothing and stop nothing. You can alter belief in two ways. Either by enlarging upon it, or by changing it completely." - Neale Donald Walsch

The Law of Belief states that whatever is in your belief system whether with feeling and conviction or not becomes your reality. It is not until you change your belief system that you can begin to change your reality and your performance. This is fact. It is not negotiable, that is the way it works. You were designed this way for very good reason, that being that you can learn through experience. The quicker you learn the easier it becomes for you.

You put them there – probably unconsciously (that is why it is called the subconscious) at some point in time. If they serve you then that is good and well. If you find that they do not serve you, then YOU need to find them, and undo them, and then put something else in their place so that they can then serve you the way you intend.

Another way to state this law is in the context of having faith. All of the religions of the world talk about one's ability to always keep faith, as being a key to happiness and success. Whether you choose to follow religious dogma or not, the Law of Belief is something which can either help you achieve success or keep you from achieving it – depending upon whether you live in accordance with the law.

You have heard the doubters and the naysayers out there who always proclaim, "I'll believe it when I see it!" In reality, it is the other way around; it is not until you believe it, that you will see it (no matter what "it" is)!

Self-limiting beliefs are perhaps the most detrimental of all thoughts, since they are programmed and continuously working in your operating system making sure you get what you want, but don't believe you can attain. There is an old saying that states, "Whether you think you can or you can't, your right!" This saying is completely congruent with the Law of Belief.

The 3 Most Common Limiting Beliefs:

1. I am not good enough.
2. I am different - so I cannot connect with others.
3. I want freedom from my troubles but it's impossible.

If you find yourself believing any of these lies about yourself, refer back to "The Immovable Center" —the key principle of this program: There is nothing wrong with you.

" **The bumblebee's wings are too small for it to fly, but the bumblebee doesn't know that... so it flies.**

THE ULTIMATE
POWER

I received a text from my former client, Jeremiah, who said, "I owe a huge debt to one of your many great talks!!! "Just make a decision". Those 4 simple words changed my life." The talk went something like this: I asked, "What is your Favorite color?" The response was Blue. I then asked, "Can I take that away from you?" No. "Can your family take that from you?" No. "Can a loss of a loved one take it from you?" No! "Why?" Because it's my favorite color. "Who chose that color?" I did. See, you chose that color and now no one and no circumstance can ever take that from you. That's the power of a decision.

Choice is the ultimate power and one of the greatest gift we possess. I also feel it's something we take for granted and do not understand how powerful we truly are because of this ability to choose.

As Quoted by Viktor Frankl, "Between stimulus and response there is a space. In that space is our power to choose our response. In our response lies our growth and our freedom." Viktor is sharing with us the power that we all possess and he tells of an amazing experience he had in the death camp at Auschwitz, Germany. The Auschwitz concentration camp was a complex of over 40 concentration and extermination camps built and operated by Nazi Germany in occupied Poland during World War II and the Holocaust.

In his famous book, "Man's Search for Meaning," he describes how he came to know the power of a decision. "Most important, do the prisoners' reactions to the singular world of the concentration camp prove that man cannot escape the influences of his surroundings? Does man have no choice of action in the face of such circumstances? We can answer these questions from experience as well as on principle. The experiences of camp life show that man does have a choice of action. There were enough examples, often of a heroic nature, which proved that apathy could be overcome, irritability suppressed. Man can preserve a vestige of spiritual freedom, of independence of mind, even in such terrible conditions of psychic and physical stress.

We who lived in concentration camps can remember the men who walked through the huts comforting others, giving away their last piece of bread. They may have been few in number, but they offer sufficient proof that everything can be taken from a man but one thing: the last of the human freedoms—to choose one's attitude in any given set of circumstances, to choose one's own way. And there were always choices to make. Every day, every hour, offered the opportunity to make a decision, a decision which determined whether you would or would not submit to those powers which threatened to rob you of your very self, your inner freedom; which determined whether or not you would become the plaything of circumstance, renouncing freedom and dignity to become molded into the form of the typical inmate...

in the final analysis it becomes clear that the sort of person the prisoner became was the result of an inner decision, and not the result of camp influences alone."

7 PRINCIPLES

OF DAILY SOBRIETY

Intro

"He who is involved in numerous details without the regulating and synthesizing element of principles is like one lost in a forest, with no direct path along which to walk amid the mass objects. He is swallowed up by the details, while the man of principles contains all details within himself: he stands outside them, as it were, and grasps them in their entirety, while the other man can only see the few that are nearest to him at the time. All things are contained in principles."

A principle is a law, something that is true and constant. It serves as the foundation for a system of belief, behavior, or for a chain of reasoning. Always working, 24/7.

While a principle is great, it is nothing without doing the work to implement it into your life. A story I like to refer to is about Kobe Bryant, the NBA star. When he was on the Lakers, they were playing the Miami Heat in Miami. It was a regular season game with no playoff implications. Towards the end of the game, the Lakers are down, Kobe is going to take the last shot to try to win the game... the clock is winding down, he goes to the left side of the key, shoots right at the buzzer and misses. Lakers lose. After the game, the NBA hosted a party on the beach for both teams and all the players went down for food and drinks. Everyone is there having a great time... everyone except Kobe. Kobe is on the court shooting that same shot he missed—1,000 times. When I think about this story, I wish I could go interview the other players on the beach. I would ask them if they wish they were as good as Kobe. I am sure most of them would say yes. But the truth is, they wouldn't because if they did, they would be inside shooting that shot instead of being on the beach celebrating and eating.

If you don't put in the work, you won't get the result. How hard are you going to work to change your life? You will be remembered because you put in the work.

The following are designed to help you take control of your sobriety, one day at a time. By following these 7 principles, you will be set up for guaranteed daily success and sobriety.

Definition

INTENT: An anticipated outcome that is intended or that guides your planned actions.

DECISION: A purposeful commitment to make up your mind to do (or not do) something.

Overview

What do you do when your alarm clock goes off in the morning? As the blaring sounds seems to rip you from your dreams, you might think:

"No way. It can't be morning already. I'm way too tired,"

"I should probably get up and exercise. Maybe just a few more minutes of sleep ...."

"I don't want to go to work today. I'm not prepared for that presentation. Maybe I should just stay home."

Maybe you roll over and hit the snooze button a couple times. Or three times. Or four times. Waiting for the last possible minute you can get up and still be on time for work.

You might even think these things and manage to drag yourself out of bed anyway. Sure, you won't be happy about it, but you'll make it to work and that's what counts, right?

In my experience, it's not good enough to just roll out of bed and into the world. You're likely to just keep rolling from there. You will roll every which way and be pushed around by addiction and self-hatred.

If you wake up in the morning and the first thing you think about is how dreadful your day is going to be — boom — you've just set your tone for the day. It's a self-fulfilling prophecy. Your day will be dreadful because that's how you've imagined it from the moment you stepped into consciousness.

Well I'm here to tell you that you can change that. You are a masterful creator and you have the power to take control of how your day goes and how well you accomplish your goals. You set the intent to wake up the moment you set your alarm. When your alarm goes off, you decide to get up and honor that intent.

You win the first hour of the day, you win the day! If you lose the first hour of the day, you will spend your whole day looking for it.

It all starts first thing in the morning when you wake up. You can choose to think negative thoughts and have a negative day; or you can take responsibility, start the day on a positive vibe, and tap into the true nature of your potential.

I like to call this setting your Intent. "Setting a true intent is a decision you make to take control of your day and life." When you say your decision out loud you speak it into existence, and when you decide to do something, you do it. Decide to start your day with intent—Pop out of bed like a piece of toast and set your day on fire!

Your brain is most open to suggestion when you first wake up in the morning. The waking mind is filled with alpha brain waves which allow your brain to receive new ideas, form belief systems, and shape your reality. Unfortunately, this is the perfect opportunity for The Bully to step in and put you down.

The problem is that so many people allow The Bully to set their Intent for them without even realizing it. They don't think about how those first precious minutes of the day have the power to change everything, and so The Bully steps in, telling them they will fail.

Fortunately, if you are conscientious about setting your Intent, the first moments of the day can provide you with the chance to drown out the voice of The Bully with positive self-talk, alter the way you feel about yourself and others, and take the first steps toward affecting real change in your life.

The first thing you need to do is write an Intent statement.

The Intent statement is a short sentence or two that will become an essential part of your morning routine. After choosing and memorizing it, it will be the first thing you utter when you wake up, thus pushing aside The Bully and creating your own future through the power of Intent.

During the dark days of my addiction to drugs and alcohol, I was miserable. Every morning I woke up thinking about how miserable I was, how worthless my life was, and how I was going to fail that day.

It is through the power of Intent that I was able to overcome my addictions and change my life. This was my Intent statement:

"I, Todd, am grateful to be clean and sober. And nothing, and no one, and no circumstance is going to change my mind today."

That was it. Every morning I stated my Intent for the day. If I could do that and nothing else, the day was a success.

Notice that my Intent statement was in the present tense. I didn't say *"I, Todd, desire to become clean and sober,"* or *"I, Todd, will be clean and sober one day."* I didn't hope for sobriety, I expected it. I stated it as if it were already fact. And in time, it became fact.

Eventually I outgrew my Intent statement. I no longer had to set my Intent to be clean and sober – I was clean and sober. It had become a part of my inner being, and nothing was going to change that.

But I didn't quit stating my Intent first thing in the morning. My statement merely evolved. Here's my Intent statement today:

"I, Todd, am going to have an epic day. I am full of energy and I am going to make everything I desire come to pass."

It's miraculous how well this works.

When you have Intent, your behavior changes. Everything you do, every thought you think, will be focused on reaching your goal. Not only your own power, but all the powers of the universe seem to conspire to make your Intent happen, and you will succeed.

You'll be amazed to find that it happens every time. I get what I intend *every* time.

How do I set my Intent?

As you craft your own Intent statement, keep in mind that it doesn't have to be lofty or complex. It just has to state what you desire and what you hope to cultivate.

One of my clients says,

"I, Aaron, am grateful for today and I am happy and energetic."

Some other examples are,

"I, Cindy, am happy and I am going to live in the moment," or

"I, Sean, am happy, calm, and beautiful."

The point of this exercise is to replace negative thoughts with positive ones and suggest to the mind that you are powerful to choose how you think and feel.

As you begin to state your Intent in the morning, say it with conviction. You have to state it as fact and really feel its truth and power behind your words.

Rolling over in bed and muttering half-heartedly, "I, Jim, ... am grateful ... to be − " is not going to cut it. As soon as that alarm goes off, you have to pop out of bed like a piece of toast. Don't hit the snooze button: it's your enemy. Declare your Intent with vigor and really, truly believe it.

I call this the **"Think, Feel, Create"** principle and it is essential to building any belief system.

As you become conscious of what your Intent is and start to state it out loud, you will begin to feel it and know it to be true. Then you will have the power to create it and make it a part of your reality.

Setting your Intent doesn't even take five minutes. It only takes five seconds, but they may be the most important five seconds of your day. This one small act has the potential to change your entire day and cause miracles to happen in your life.

Your Intent is your defense against The Bully—All day long

First waking up in the morning may be the most important part of your day, but don't let your Intent stop there! You should find yourself re-stating your Intent several times throughout the day.

The Bully is relentless. He won't rest until you've caved or cracked − given in to old habits or surrendered your power − and he will keep haranguing you all day long.

In the past this may have seemed intimidating, but once you have set your Intent you don't have to fear The Bully. He has no power over you. Your Intent statement will become your sword and shield with which you will fend off The Bully. It's your comeback for any time he tries to put you down.

During the first years of my sobriety, whenever I had the urge to use or drink alcohol I could simply say, "Nice try. I'm not falling for that one. I, Todd, am grateful to be clean and sober..." etc.

And that was all I had to do. I knew what my Intent was because I had already defined it. All I had to do at that point was decide to stick to it.

Remember the three foundational belief principles that constitute Love of Self:

1. I have the dignity to choose
2. I am a masterful creator
3. I am powerful beyond measure

When you set your Intent, you are demonstrating your ability to choose. Don't let yourself be a victim of The Bully. If you do, you are only becoming a victim of yourself. Take responsibility for the way you feel instead. Create your own fulfilling reality, and watch as your Intent fills you with power.

Write your personal intent and decision statement

Now it is your turn! Take a minute to reflect on your biggest adversary, the thing you need to face daily. Then think of some positive and encouraging statements you could make a part of your intent and decision statement to get you out of bed and keep you motivated. (Remember, your intent should be stated in the present tense.)

EXAMPLES:

◆ I Todd am grateful to be clean and sober and nothing and no one and no circumstance with change my mind today!
◆ I Todd am full of energy and today is going to wonderful!
◆ I don't hope for success today, I demand it!
◆ I Todd (State any of the 3 Foundational principles.)

_____
_____
_____
_____
_____
_____
_____
_____

DECLARE

Definition

DECLARE: To make known as a determination. Acknowledging that you already possess something.

Overview

One of the fastest and more effective ways to develop a new belief system is with the Personal Declaration Statement.

For the past 20 years, I have started off almost every single day with a Personal Declaration Statement. I read this to myself with conviction right after I set my Intent for the day.

The Personal Declaration Statement is a living document that you modify often—it represents your hopes, goals, dreams, and a listing of who you are at your core. The Personal Declaration Statement is the TRUTH of you.

When you read this Statement each day, you are shutting down the voice of The Bully.

Imagine when The Bully starts telling you in the afternoon:

"I am tired – I need an energy drink"

What happens when you hear this voice? You probably go grab an energy drink!

If you have already read your Personal Declaration Statement for the day, you may have said:

"I am FULL of energy today!"

So now, when that thought about the energy drink comes in your mind, you can go right back to your Personal Declaration Statement and you'll remember...

"Oh yeah, I don't need an energy drink, because I am FULL of energy today!"

I know, it sounds so simple—that's because it is!

Finding Your Why

The hardest part of creating a Declaration Statement might be deciding what exactly it is you stand for. The task of condensing all of your life's purpose into a few well-thought-out paragraphs is daunting to say the least.

Alternatively, some of you may be struggling with addictions, anxiety, or other challenges. It may feel like a lack of direction in life is causing you to feel down and depressed or that your goals are too far out of reach.

Sorry to take away your excuses, but it's not true. You are powerful beyond measure and are free to choose, not only how you feel, but what direction your life takes. The only person who can stop you from making your desires become reality is you.

That being said, here are a couple of strategies to help you overcome your writer's block and get started on your Declaration Statement.

- ◆ Remember that this is not the final draft. It's just for you so while it should be thoughtful, it doesn't need to be perfect.

- ◆ It's okay if you don't know exactly what you want out of life just yet. Just write what you feel right now and the rest will come as you start living by the principles you're learning

Now, let's try a technique I call Limitless Wishing.

Start by closing your eyes and imagining that your life has no limits, no boundaries, and no restrictions. Take some time to let all your fears and apprehensions slip away. Then, write down everything you would wish for on the lines below. Don't think about it too much, just let it pour out of your mind and onto the page.

_____

_____

_____

_____

_____

_____

_____

_____

_____

_____

_____

The next step is perhaps the most important. You must look at what you wrote down and ask yourself: why? This is the key to unlocking what really matters to you in life.

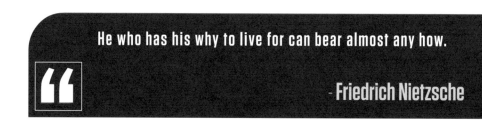

He who has his why to live for can bear almost any how.

- Friedrich Nietzsche

If you wished for lots of money, you should ask yourself why that is. It might be so that you can help lots of people and give to charity. It might be so that you can have the luxury of pursuing a passion like scholarship or music. It might simply be that you desire the financial security of knowing the basic needs of your family will be met.

Whatever the reason, the why reveals something crucial about your inner self. This will help you to form an image of yourself that you can strive for—one that you can write down and confidently state each morning as truth.

Creating Your Own Personal Declaration Statement

If you were to die tomorrow, how would people remember you? Who would attend your funeral? What songs would be sung? What words would appear on your headstone? Would you have become everything you wanted to be?

All this is not to seem ominous. You probably won't die tomorrow (I certainly hope you don't) and all these details may seem far away in the future.

This exercise can be helpful in considering what you stand for in life. Nothing is as powerful in determining your destiny as what you believe and what you want to become. It defines the very core of your being.

Here is an example of a Personal Declaration Statement from a good friend and client of mine so you can get an idea of what it looks like:

I, (NAME), am going to have an epic day! I inspire and motivate those around me! I am actively completing the things that are both important short term AND long term. I am full of energy, have a clear mind, have plenty of time to complete my projects and feel healthy inside and out.

I, (NAME), am a masterful creator. I create products and services that provide huge value to the people I work with

I have the ability to choose. I CHOOSE to create energy, warmth, acceptance, productivity and good vibes

I am powerful beyond measure. I can create ANYTHING I set my mind on and I constantly tap into the divine power around me.

I, (NAME), am wealthy with positive monthly cash flow. I have a strong, healthy savings account and I make the investments I want. I drive the cars I want, live in the house I want, wear what I want, travel where I want, and am very generous with my friends and in the community.

I am a loyal friend! I am kind to everyone. I am filled with light, knowledge and power. God, the creator of all things, is my Father and my personal mentor. He teaches me daily how to tap into inspiration and attract all good things. As I do this, I can create ANYTHING.

I am one of the most highly sought-after personalities, leaders, and individuals. Companies apply to work with me and investors, venture capital and private equity groups seek me out and ask for my opinions.

I have amazing relationships with my wife and my family. I constantly go above and beyond with my wife and we have a legendary relationship—full of love and growth. I bring love and understanding, acceptance, and compassion into every interaction I have. I am filled with love always.

I am a good person.

As you can see, his intention statement is very specific to him and what he is working on. As different projects and priorities come up, he may add them in and some stuff may change. But in the end, the ideas in here are universal, long-lasting principles.

Here are a few tips to keep in mind as your build your own Personal Declaration Statement:

- Go big. You are Ghandi, Alexander the Great, Einstein.
- No limits. If you had endless supply of money, power, and potential, what would you do with your time?
- Guess what? You do!
- Give it time. This is a living document. Let it grow and change
- Ask others. Choose a few people you trust to help you see who you truly are and what you have to offer the world.
- Build your dream. Don't hold anything back. Don't be ashamed to have material thoughts and desires.
- You deserve health, wealth, and happiness!

> Once you decide to do something, the whole universe conspires to make it happen.

 Assignment

Personal Declaration Statement Creation

So, what's next? Get going! Using your why from above, write your first draft of your Personal Declaration Statement. Remember this is a living document that will grow and change as you progress.

_____

_____

_____

_____

_____

_____

_____

_____

_____

_____

_____

_____

_____

_____

_____

_____

_____

_____

_____

_____

_____

_____

_____

_____

_____

_____

_____

_____

_____

_____

After you have written your first draft, it is time to put it into action.

- ◆ Wake in the morning, set, and state your Intent
- ◆ Read your Personal Declaration Statement out loud. (You can keep it somewhere close by in paper form or save it electronically.)
- ◆ When you are done, you should be able to say, "I know who I am, I know what I want, and believe in and I am willing to die for it."

You will love the extra power you will have each day as you read your Personal Declaration Statement. Remember, you need to read it with power and conviction.

This is your plan A. There is no plan B. If you have a plan B, plan A will never happen. Plan A is your Intent, Decision, and Declaration. Nothing is going to stop you from moving forward.

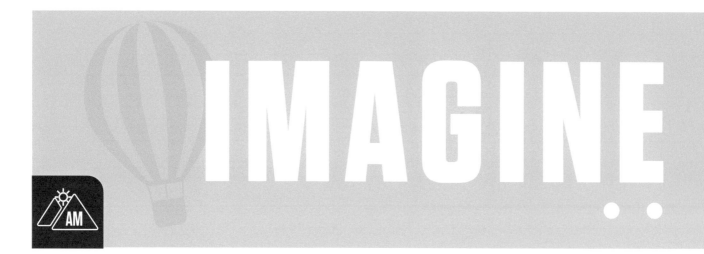

IMAGINE

Definition

IMAGINE: To form a mental image of something not present.

Overview

You probably know that Olympic athletes spend hours a day training for their events. What you might not know is that they equally spend hours a day imagining. Expert athletes know that visualizing the execution of their sport is as important as the practice itself. They will close their eyes and imagine performing their event perfectly several times each day.

It's important that they feel and experience the event in vivid color. They will picture every minute detail as if they were actually there, as if it were real. They will see the sights and hear the sounds.

A downhill skier will feel the cold wind and smell the clean alpine air. He will feel the gate hit his leg and the snow push against his skis as he launches himself downhill. He'll hear the cowbell in the audience, the crowd cheering. He will feel the wind rush past his face as he tears across the finish line with a record-breaking time.

He'll even visualize standing up on the podium after the event. He'll hear the sound of his national anthem being played and feel the weight of the gold medal being placed around his neck. Some athletes imagine this and feel the emotions so strongly that it moves them to tears.

The reason for this is that the brain doesn't know the difference between a real event and an imagined one. Your mind can fool itself into thinking that your imagined experiences are actually happening.

Because of this, Imagination can be a powerful tool to make your hopes and desires a reality. Athletes use it to replicate the experience of being a champion and prepare their minds to handle executing their events perfectly.

You, too, can use Imagination to visualize your life going exactly how you want it to. This will make it easier for you to go out into the world and make your visualizations come true.

THE SCIENCE OF IMAGINATION

In psychology and social studies, picturing imagined events as reality has been called many things: confabulation, imagination inflation, and synthetic experience, to name a few.

When a mind blurs the lines too much between imagination and reality, mental health specialists often diagnose an illness such as schizophrenia, dissociative identity disorder, or delusional disorder.

I am not suggesting that these diagnoses are false, nor that you lose your grip on reality. On the contrary, I am saying that a healthy dose of Imagination can help make your dream a reality. This is a claim which scientific studies support.

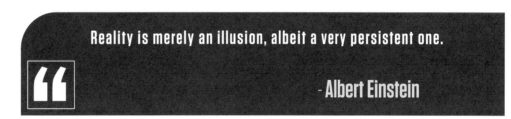

Reality is merely an illusion, albeit a very persistent one.

- Albert Einstein

One study published in American Psychologist discusses how the imagination can be harnessed to bring about positive events in the future. Through what lead researcher Shelley Taylor calls "mental simulation," subjects were more likely to accomplish their future goals, handle stress and anxiety, and improve their lives.

The actual act of Imagination had a much more powerful effect on the research subjects than just reading positive words in self-help books (Again, I'd like to emphasize the importance of putting in the work and following the steps I've given you).

Additionally, researchers have found that imagination improves memory, and can even help repair neurological damage.

I personally can vouch for the positive effects of Imagination. I have witnessed it perform miracles, not only in my own life, but in the lives of many clients who have sought to change their belief system.

After Declaring, you should spend 5-10 minutes visualizing your desires coming into being. You can spend part of this time playing out your day in your head, picturing that each event happens exactly as you want it and you live up to your Intent.

If you have an important meeting at work, you can picture every detail going exactly as planned. If you have an exam at school, imagine being calm and answering every question correctly with ease.

You should imagine how you will say no to The Bully that day. If you will come into contact with drugs or alcohol that day, visualize how you will be strong and put The Bully back in his place. If you have to do something scary, you can Imagine overcoming anxiety, feeling relaxed, and joyful.

Your visualization should also consist of how you will become the person you describe in your declaration statement. Imagine the actions you will take, the milestones you'll reach. Imagine yourself as exactly the person you hope to create. This is your opportunity to take the future and bring it into the present.

YOU'VE IMAGINED. NOW GO CREATE IT.

When you spend your time imagining, I find it's helpful to close your eyes. You can lie down, sit up, or remain standing — whatever feels most comfortable for you!

The important part is that you really get into it and picture the events as if they were actually happening. Feel it with every ounce of your being. Like an Olympic athlete, you should imagine every detail with all of your five senses.

As you're imagining, remember your ultimate purpose. After visualizing your ideal life, you need to go out into the world and make it a reality. The power is within you to create whatever you want in your own life.

Imagination without creation is like a sail without wind. It has all the potential in the world, but it won't get anywhere. You need to give your imagined experiences life by creating them in the real world.

Don't feel intimidated by this. I know it may seem like creating in the real world is going to be more difficult than imagining in your own home, but I assure you it's not. Trust me on this one.

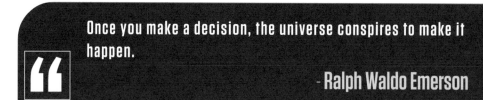

Once you make a decision, the universe conspires to make it happen.

- Ralph Waldo Emerson

You'll find as you start Imagining, that opportunities will arise for you to take your desires and create them into reality. It's like they come out of nowhere. It's like magic.

Maybe the Universe is rewarding you for having a positive outlook on life, or maybe the opportunities were always there but now you have the the insight to recognize them and the courage to take them. Either way, your morning Imagination is a crucial step in your preparation to receive all the Universe has to offer you.

The Universe always says "yes". If say that you want to be positive, happy, and full of energy, that's exactly what you're going to get.

The opposite is also true.

If you are constantly sending out signals that you are depressed, powerless, scared, and helpless, that's exactly what the Universe is going to throw back at you.

Take anxiety for example. Anxiety is nothing more than a misuse of the imagination.

When you are anxious about something, you are choosing to imagine something that is false. You are worrying about a future event that won't ever happen. This is called Future Tripping. The only way it can happen is if you keep visualizing it as the truth. As long as you imagine a beautiful and positive reality, you have NOTHING to be anxious about.

Your Imagination Rules the World.

- Dennis Waitley

Assignment

Spend 5-10 minutes imagining your declaration statement in vivid detail. Make this your daily mental workout routine:

- Get relaxed
- Turn on meditation music in the background
- Focus on your breathing for 5 minutes, then spend 5 minutes imagining your declaration statement

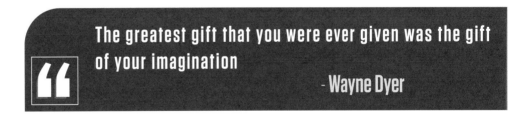

The greatest gift that you were ever given was the gift of your imagination

- Wayne Dyer

HOUR OF POWER CHALLENGE

If you have an hour in the morning to dedicate to yourself, I recommend practicing my Hour of Power routine. It is similar to the daily assignment above but I dedicate a whole hour to it and there are some additional steps. The first few steps you have already learned about. Here is what my Hour of Power consists of:

◆ I put on some soft meditation music and start with a prayer, you can also start with setting your intention for this next hour.

◆ I create my Intent and Decision for the day.

◆ I read my Personal Declaration Statement.

◆ I imagine for 5 minutes my Personal Declaration in detail.

◆ I read from the book titled, "Mind is the Master" by James Allen (30 min.) He is my hero and he started the self-help movement back in 1903. I will read a page or two from this book and ponder what it means to me. I then commit to living it today and sharing it with all my clients I have in sessions for the day. The quality of the books you read matters.

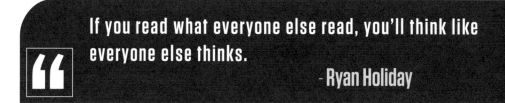

> **If you read what everyone else read, you'll think like everyone else thinks.**
> — Ryan Holiday

◆ I embrace the silence for 5-15 minutes. This is where God, the Universe speaks to my soul. This is the end of suffering! In Psalms 46:10 it states, be still and know that I am God. I keep a pad of paper and pen next to me. When inspiration comes to me, I write it down.

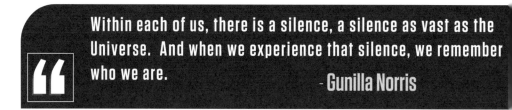

> **Within each of us, there is a silence, a silence as vast as the Universe. And when we experience that silence, we remember who we are.**
> — Gunilla Norris

◆ I end my Hour of Power by giving it away. There is a principle that I teach and have lived by for over 25 years now. "If you want to be...Give it away." This is a game changer. If I want to be inspiring, I will give it away to someone today. I will inspire someone today. I will write a letter of appreciation, text a friend, plan an act of greatness for the day, etc. When I give it away, I am declaring that I have it! Then, God, the Universe answers with a resounding YES! It's a beautiful thing.

All the greats have one common thread, they all get up early and work on themselves.
- Todd Sylvester

My experience waking up at 4 AM, popping out of bed like a piece of toast and doing an Hour of Power, I have witnessed first-hand, life changing blessings. Doing this consistently takes away fear, anxiety, depression, guilt, shame, sadness, despair, and self-hatred. It also creates love, joy, enlightenment, power, energy, gratitude, self-discipline, resilience, thoroughness, and a powerful mind set. It opens my heart to the truth that what I focus on increases.

It also helps me stay firm on the immovable principle, that you are okay! That there is nothing wrong with you and there never was. It eliminates all inward conflict. It takes care of restlessness uncertainty and sorrow. It puts me in a position to be connected with the infinite field, the law of attraction becomes real and noticeable. I am more calm, centered and productive. Life seems good and good things seem to flow to me throughout my day. There is an increase of harmony and insight growing in my soul. It truly lights my soul on fire!

GREATNESS

Definition

GREATNESS: Greatness is refusing the drugs or alcohol when no one is around. Greatness is doing the right thing.

Overview

You may have heard of the "random act of kindness." I would like to upgrade it to a "Random Act of Greatness."

The difference is that acts of Greatness go beyond just putting a smile on someone's face or making their day better. By helping others, acts of Greatness also build and fortify the actor. Both people will grow together in Greatness. Part of Greatness is owning who you are and what you stand for.

You need to be proud of the changes you are making in your life and feel no shame for how the world views your changes. Greatness is being passionate about who you are, not being afraid to talk about it with other people, and not letting anyone stand in your way of being great.

Do an Act of Greatness Everyday

OWNING IT

One of the hardest parts of becoming sober was breaking the news to my friends. Some of these guys had been my friends since elementary school, and during that time they had developed an image of what they thought I stood for in life.

I can tell you, it wasn't much.

Still, it was difficult telling my friends that I wouldn't be joining them on the party scene anymore. I was worried about what they might think of me. Would they still think I was fun? Would they think that I wasn't who they thought I was?

In retrospect, I hope they did notice I had changed. I wasn't the same person they had known growing up, and I am proud to have become who I am today.

Part of Greatness is owning who you are and what you stand for.

You need to be proud of the changes you are making in your life and feel no shame for how the world views your changes. Greatness is being passionate about who you are, not being afraid to talk about it with other people, and not letting anyone stand in your way of being great.

I won't lie to you, you will face resistance as you start to discover your new power. It's the unfortunate paradox of positive change. Negative people thrive on negative energy and they will try to make you doubt the power of positive change.

Handling these situations requires a delicate balance. Your ultimate goal should be not only to maintain your own love of self, but to share that love with others around you.

Be proud, but not arrogant. Try to maintain your positive attitude without letting negative people stomp on you. It may take some time for you to get the hang of dealing with negative people, and that's okay.

The thing is, as you are proud about the changes you make in your behaviour, eventually those changes will become a part of who you are. People who know you will also change how they view you and how they act towards you.

Your friends will stop offering you drugs and alcohol because they'll already know: "That's Todd. He doesn't do that stuff." And if your friends are true friends, they'll respect you for it.

Owning your problems and also owning the solution will make you stronger. You'll become fortified against The Bully and have more power to shrug off his attacks throughout the day.

DOING WHAT'S RIGHT WHEN NO ONE ELSE IS AROUND

Great boxers are lauded for their outstanding achievements in the ring. They fight before thousands of spectators, sometimes millions through pay-per-view. They hold titles, belts, and some can even boast that they are undefeated.

What some people forget is that a boxer's real achievements don't take place in the ring. Titles are won beforehand when boxers train entirely on their own.

Successful boxers get up early in the morning. They run, they jump rope, they hit the bags. They box against the only person keeping them from the title, themselves.

All this time there's no ring, no roaring crowd, no bell. Just the boxer and him or herself.

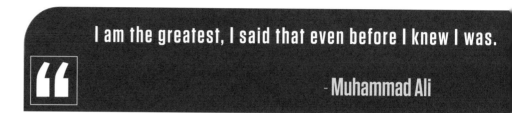

I am the greatest, I said that even before I knew I was.

- Muhammad Ali

Discipline will be your most important ally as you face up to your problems. No one is going to make you change your behaviors because they can't. Not a friend, not a spouse, not even God. The only person who can change you is you.

True Greatness is choosing to do what's best for you even when nobody's watching you.

I can tell you right now the difference between people who are successful in recovery and those who aren't. Successful people do their homework. They Set their Intent in the morning. They write their Declaration Statement.

It's one thing to learn these principles but it's another to actually do them. If you don't put in the work when nobody's there to make you do it, you'll never succeed.

This principle applies especially to the internal battles you will fight throughout the day. You're going to have to take on The Bully alone. No one will know when he is beating you down and trying to make you doubt who you really are. Greatness is sticking it to The Bully, even when it's just him and you.

These victories over The Bully can be very simple. I asked one of my clients, Madison, to describe herself in a phrase that was the opposite of how she really felt about herself. She said, "I, Madison, am an extraordinary person." It was sad that she felt that way, but it gave her a target to shoot for. She had to become extraordinary.

One day while at work, Madison was moving something in the back of her office and caused a filing box to fall covering the floor with papers. Her initial reaction was to leave the papers where they were. No one would know it was her who toppled the box.

But then something changed. She said to herself: "No. I, Madison, am an extraordinary person, and an extraordinary person would pick up the box." She then proceeded to gather the papers and put the box back on the shelf.

Greatness is in the small things. It's picking up the box. It's small victories every day that have the power to change who we really are.

GREATNESS MEANS STANDING ALONE

Part of Greatness is doing what's right for you even when it's the hardest thing to do. Sometimes, that means ending unhealthy relationships.

In my first years of sobriety, I said goodbye to many friends. It's not that I thought I was better than them, it's just that I couldn't afford to be around people who helped me justify falling into negative habits. The truth is, I would rather be alone and sober than have friends and be miserable.

Many people use their relationships as a source of negative validation. They might seek people out who will coddle them and feed into their anxiety. They might use fights and arguments in their relationships as an excuse to drink or use drugs.

In my experience, toxic relationships are the number one reason for people to relapse. I've know clients who don't even go home after rehab because they are aware of the enabling power of their destructive relationships.

Now I'm not saying that you should immediately go out and cut ties with everyone you know. Good relationships do have the potential to be a positive force in your life. I'm saying that you need to learn how to identify bad relationships and be prepared to stand alone when necessary.
Trust me, you will know whether a relationship is healthy or not.

You may be concerned about being alone, but there's no reason to be worried. Like attracts like. As you go on changing your lifestyle,new friends will gravitate toward you. You will find like-minded people who share your outlook on life and build you up rather than tearing you down.

I don't expect anyone to spend their life alone, but a willingness to stand on your own two legs is a quality of true Greatness.

The two most important days of a person's life is the day they were born and the day they found out why.

- Mark Twain

A CUPFUL OF LEMONADE. A HANDFUL OF CHANGE.

I was driving home from work when I passed a little girl's lemonade stand. After stopping and buying a cup, I spontaneously scooped all of the coins that had accumulated in my car's cup holder and gave it to this young entrepreneur. Her face lit up like... well, like a child who had unexpectedly been given a handful of pocket change.

It was such a simple act. I hadn't accomplished anything difficult or noble. I had merely done something small for someone else. And in return, everything inside of me was changing. It was as if a dam that had been holding back a decade of guilt, depression, and sadness had suddenly broken free. Soon, I found myself pulling my car to the side of the road because I was sobbing uncontrollably.

For nearly ten years, my life had been controlled by my addictions. I had felt powerless, a victim of my circumstances. But after making the tiny decision to give this young girl my cup full of change – and seeing the excitement and gratitude that it brought her – I understood that I still had the power to make my own choices – even if, at the moment, they were still small choices.

And for the first time since I had developed my addictions, I began to see that if I stopped focusing on myself and my need for drugs, I could stop the negative thoughts that had been dominating my mind and heart. If I stopped focusing inward – on my own unhappiness and self-centered desire to feed my own addiction – and started focusing on others, I could find true happiness.

I share my "lemonade story" often because it was so pivotal to my recovery. It was a breakthrough, a catalyst. It wasn't just a moment. This was the moment when everything inside of me began to click into place.

One activity that I have my clients do is write a letter about what they think Greatness means to someone they care about. I then have the client read the letter to me and ultimately send it out. It's fascinating to see their responses.

I had Sarah, one of my clients, try out this activity when she was having arguments with her sister. Sarah's sister was angry with her for relapsing and winding up back in rehab.

When Sarah had written her letter and I told her to send it to her sister, she was shocked. I guess she thought the writing process was supposed to be therapeutic, but she didn't intend to actually send the letter.

I managed to convince her to send the letter anyway and the result was astounding.

Her sister was in tears. She had taken Sarah's letter, laminated it, and put in on her wall. "I'm going to read it every day," she told Sarah. Sarah's random act of Greatness had healing effect on her relationship with her sister.

That's what acts of Greatness are for. Your acts should help lift, and inspire others.

> **If you're not making someone else's life better, then you're wasting your time.**
>
> — Will Smith

By making the lives of others great, you will become great yourself. Your life will become better, fuller, and you will experience more joy.

Assignment

Sit down and make a list of people who you want to make an impact on in your life. Who do you want to feel the power of Greatness?

_____

_____

_____

_____

_____

_____

_____

_____

_____

This isn't something you will do daily, but the assignment is to write a Greatness Letter to a loved one, read it to them (if you can) then give it to them to keep. (If you only have the option to mail it, that is fine too.)

> **The most powerful weapon on earth is the human soul on fire.**
>
> — Ferdinand Foch

> **Greatness is not something that if you meet it once it stays with you forever...It will require sustaining greatness for a long period of time...it will demand singular focus and may upset the balance of your life**
>
> — David Goggins
> *You Can't Hurt Me*

GRATITUDE

EVENING

Definition

GRATITUDE: The quality of being thankful.

LAW OF ATTRACTION: The attractive, magnetic power of the Universe that draws similar energies together.

Overview

Are you a Miracle?

Here's a thought—What's the probability of you being born? In a recent talk at TEDx San Francisco, Mel Robbins, a self-help author, mentioned that scientists estimate the probability of your being born at about one in 400 trillion. Wow!

A miracle is an event so unlikely as to be almost impossible. By that definition, I've just proven that you are a miracle.

Now go forth and feel and act like the miracle that you are.

We live on a blue planet that circles a ball of fire next to a moon that controls the seas and we think miracles don't happen?

GRATITUDE AND THE LAW OF ATTRACTION

I am a firm believer in the Law of Attraction. This is a new belief that simply states, "like attracts like." If you send out negativity into the Universe, that's exactly what you're going to get back. Positivity pulls in positivity. Goodness gravitates toward goodness.

This truth is powerful when you consider the importance of Gratitude. Being Grateful puts you in a place of abundance rather than scarcity. The more Gratitude you have, the more you will have to be Grateful for!

> **Acknowledging the good that you already have in your life is the foundation for all abundance.**
>
> **- Eckhart Tolle**

To someone who is used to seeing the bad in life rather than the good, this may seem backwards. "Give me something to be grateful for and then I will have gratitude," they might say. I can assure you that while this way of thinking seems logical, it is false. It's like saying to the stove, "Give me heat, then I will put in wood."

If you spend all your life waiting for something good to happen to you, *you will spend all your life waiting for something good to happen to you.* The good will never come. Waiting, wishing, and scarcity beget more waiting, wishing, and scarcity.

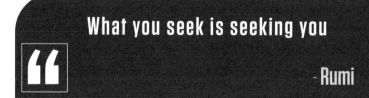

> **What you seek is seeking you**
>
> **- Rumi**

The contrary is true as well. If you focus on the good in your life and appreciate it, you start seeing good in more and more places – places you never thought to look.

Not only will your perceptions change, but more good things will happen to you. Grateful people are joyful, positive, and more attractive. Goodness comes their way, the Universe blesses them, and when opportunity knocks, Grateful people are prepared to recognize and act on it.

Just think: what if God only gave you today the things that you were grateful for yesterday? How would that change what things you notice in your life? The truth is, we have SO much and we rarely take the time to appreciate it.

It's like comedian Louis CK said on Conan:

"Everything is amazing, and nobody's happy!"

"We live in an amazing, amazing world and it's wasted on the crappiest generation of spoiled idiots."

"On planes, people come back from flights and they tell you their story, and it's a horror story they act like their flight was like a cattle car from the '40s in Germany. That's how bad they make it sound.

"People talk about delays on flights? New York to California in 5 hours. That used to take 30 YEARS!"

Be grateful for your hardships

It should be apparent by now that the world is filled with things to be Grateful for — and hopefully appreciating the good things is starting to become easy. Something much harder, but equally important, is learning to appreciate your hardships, worries, and challenges. This might sound crazy, but it's actually one of the most essential parts of Gratitude.

No matter your circumstance, all of us face hard times that really make us question all of the good things in our lives. It always seems that just when life is going really well and everything is coming together, something comes along and knocks the wind out of us.

For some reason, negative experiences always seem to outweigh good experiences on our cosmic scale. They make us blind to all the good things that surround us. This is exactly the attitude that you need to change if you want to truly experience Love of Self. You can arrive at a place where trials make up your Gratitude list.

It's not so much being Grateful for the bad things in your life as learning to find the good in every hardship, trial, and tragedy. It's realizing that hardships actually have the power to make us stronger and teach us more about who we really are.

As I look back at my addiction, all I can feel is immense and overwhelming gratitude. It's allowed me to help other people. It's made me stronger. It's made me who I am.

Don't get me wrong, it was the hardest, darkest, most miserable time of my life. There were days where I felt like there was NOTHING I could do to change my life and get better. At one point I felt that the only way to escape misery was evacuating this life all together. But it didn't end that way. I survived to look back at the experience and feel gratitude.

And I can tell you right now, while there were moments like the Lemonade Stand where I had breakthroughs, times when I felt the voice of God calling me back into the fold, ultimately there was nothing that violently pulled me from my pains, no deus ex machina ending.

Likewise, you can't wait for your problems to be over for you to start living! You may look forward to the day that you can look back on your problems and appreciate them for the lessons they taught you. My counsel for you is: make that day today!

You can start appreciating your hardships today. I know it's difficult, but trust me, it's worth it. With Gratitude, there's nothing too hard, no trial you can't overcome. Gratitude is acceptance. It's taking whatever comes your way and finding the good in it. You can't truly be grateful for your blessings unless you learn to appreciate your trials.

What Gratitude will do for your life

As you make Gratitude a bigger part of your everyday life, you will notice that it changes your perspective on everything. Things that you used to find difficult will become a delight. Tragedies will become valuable learning experiences. Your life will be full, abundant, and joyous.

Just consider the way little children think.

As young children we were grateful for everything. Rather than griping and focusing on the things we don't have, we were fascinated by the littlest things.

You know what I'm talking about if you've ever seen a child in a room full of expensive toys who chooses to play with something like a length of string or a piece of paper. Children see the good in everything in their path. They love EVERYTHING.

Poor children in Africa and other developing regions may receive something as meager as a single bowl of rice and beans as their food for the day.

Do you want to know the difference between a child in the U.S. and a child in Africa? The child in the U.S. despises the meal. They complain about the quality of food, about eating the same thing for dinner every day. The child in Africa loves the bowl. They see it as a bountiful feast and are grateful for the food that they do receive. And guess what. They're happier.

The difference between famine and feast is all about Gratitude. It's the same bowl of rice in each case, but the beholder has changed.

You are powerful beyond measure and deserve to have every good thing in this life. But do you know the best way to get it? By learning to see the good in every part of life. If you learn to be Grateful, there's no way you can ever be miserable.

How to be grateful

By now you have learned about Intent, the Personal Declaration Statement, and Imagination. These three acts have given you a morning routine which will fortify you against The Bully and give you the tools you need to become a Masterful Creator.

Now I will give you a series of actions to perform sometime before you go to bed. These actions will help you reflect on your day, celebrate your successes, and find ways you'd like to improve.

The first step in this routine is to list three things you are Grateful for and why. In order to access the power to create whatever we want in our lives, we first need to learn to be grateful for what we already have.

Whether you are recovering from an addiction, overcoming depression, or simply wish to better yourself and witness positive change in your life, there may be times when you feel low. There may be times throughout your day when The Bully gets the best of you, things that don't go your way.

By listing three things you're Grateful for at the end of the day, you remind yourself of all the good that's in your life. Given this perspective, The Bully seems small and insignificant. His attacks pale in comparison to the abundance of good that comes your way every single day.

Keep in mind that this process is different from the traditional practice of counting your blessings instead of sheep. You don't need to be Grateful for a long, extensive list of things. In fact, I want you to focus on just three things and really dig into what makes you Grateful for them. Don't worry, there's plenty of time throughout the day to be Grateful for every one of your blessings

The real power in this exercise comes through the why. It's one thing to say you're Grateful for your health, but asking yourself why really drives it home. You will discover all the doors that your health opens for you.

You have the ability to work, run, and play. You don't have to pay expensive medical fees. You can go the places you want to go and do the things you want to do. You save your loved ones from the heartache of seeing you ill and incapacitated.

In essence, your health, in whatever measure of good health you have, is miraculous.

As you spend time each night appreciating the good in your life and pondering how vastly those things impact your life, you will begin to realize the abundance that you really have. This abundance will become a powerful force as it draws more and more from the Universe's well of goodness.

Gratitude List

Write down below all the things you are grateful for and why. Be very descriptive.

GRATITUDE LIST

_____   _____

_____   _____

_____   _____

_____   _____

_____   _____

_____   _____

_____   _____

_____   _____

_____   _____

_____   _____

_____   _____

_____   _____

_____   _____

_____   _____

Gratitude is the most powerful stimulate on the planet.

HONESTY

Definition

HONESTY: The quality of being honest. "Relapse killer"

Overview

THE DESTRUCTION OF DECEIT

I have watched thousands of people make huge changes in their lives, go from depression to immense joy. Then some of them return to self-hatred like a dog to its vomit. Why? How do people, after tasting what it's really like to start living, choose to go back to a life of misery?

It starts with a simple lie—a justification.

People who relapse use some aspect of their circumstances to fabricate a reason to return to their addiction or anxiety. It could be losing a job, a family problem, tragedy, or other disruption.

Tragedies are real and it's only natural to feel sorrow, but you can't let that sorrow kick you off the wagon. First of all, as I said about Gratitude, you should try to see the good in tragedies and try to learn from the experience. Second, using the tragedy as a justification for bad behavior is ALWAYS dishonest.

Take the death of a loved one for example. When a loved one dies an addict might tell himself: "It's too hard"

There's the lie right there.

I'm not saying that the death of a loved one isn't hard. Of course it is? I'm saying that it's not "too hard." If you're honest with yourself, you will know that there's nothing too difficult for you to handle. You have the dignity and capacity to choose. Of course you will feel pain for a time, but you will move forward and become stronger for it.

If you say that you relapsed because of a certain event in your life, that's a lie! It's a justification. Nothing can force you to do something that's bad for you. However, if you become fully Honest with yourself, you will catch these little lies before they have the power to take you down.

I once had a client named Blake who had been sober for 6 months when he relapsed. Hard.

He had gotten himself so messed up one night that someone had called 911 and the paramedics had to come and get him. When I asked him what happened he said, "I told myself I could handle just one beer." That was it. That was the simple, seemingly harmless lie that brought down a man who hadn't had a drink in 6 months.

If you really think about it, you'll find that what I say is true. Every relapse, every negative act, begins with a lie about who you are and what you stand for. It's telling yourself you're powerless when really you are powerful beyond measure. It's telling yourself you're a victim when you actually have the ability to choose.

Keep in mind that you can't ever be Honest with yourself if you are not Honest with those around you. The two go hand in hand. If I'm lying to someone, I'm lying to myself.

Being dishonest with your friends and family can seriously cripple your attempts to recover, whether from personal addiction, anxiety and depression, or any other negative belief system. I've even had family members of addicts tell me that the lies hurt them and their family more than the bad behavior itself.

By being Honest with yourself and others, you will come to know the truth about who you really are. The Bully can't touch you.

POWER IN TELLING THE TRUTH

Honesty is a whole lot more than just not lying. It's TELLING THE TRUTH.

It's not enough to just dutifully avoid lying, and yet, remain silent. You need to passionately declare the truth to yourself and everyone around you. There's real power in boldly stating the things you know to be true.

Telling the truth should begin first thing in the morning when you wake up and set your Intent. By saying, "I, (Name), am going to have an epic day," you make it true. You speak it into existence. The same can be said for your Personal Declaration Statement and Imagination exercises.

Throughout the day The Bully will try to get you to lie to yourself.

- ◆ "It's too hard"
- ◆ "I'm just not feeling it today"
- ◆ "There's nothing I can do"

You need to combat these lies by instead stating the powerful truths you have learned over the course of these lessons:

- "I can do anything I wish to"
- "I am full of love and energy"
- "I am a good person"
- "I have the freedom to choose"
- "I am a masterful creator"
- "I am powerful beyond measure"

As you become an emissary of the truth, you will begin to realize that you are okay. This is a powerful truth I tell my clients all the time. You're okay!

I had a client who was having a rough time. She was struggling just to get through the day because of depression. On several occasions she came close to using drugs again rather than going through the day feeling "not okay."

Then I told her the truth, "You are okay!"

"Today doesn't have to be bad, Sarah. You can make it whatever you want it to be. You. Are. Okay."

Honesty is vulnerability, and that's what makes it so difficult for people to be Honest with themselves and others. They don't want to have to feel emotions, so they hide behind the lies they tell themselves.

But feeling is one of the most important steps to recovery! Feeling is what takes your thoughts, hopes, and desires and brings them into reality. You have to FEEL to CREATE. Make the decision right now that you will be willing to feel emotion, willing to be vulnerable, and willing to be totally and completely Honest.

Honesty should be your passion. It should be something that fills your mind every day and consumes your every action.

Try to be like Honest Abe! According to his wife, Mary Todd Lincoln, Abraham Lincoln was "almost a monomaniac on the subject of honesty." This means that he was Honest nearly to the point of obsession.

You never have to remember what you said if you are always honest.

I know it sounds extreme but it's necessary. If you're anything like I was when I was 22, you probably have a lot of catching up to do. Most of us have years and years of experience in deceiving ourselves and others. By fixating on being Honest, you can repair that damage and start to experience the power of truth telling.

By shifting your focus to Honesty, I can guarantee that you will experience life in a whole new way. It's extraordinarily liberating to know that you are completely Honest, that you have nothing to hide, no skeletons in the closet.

It's possible that you have never felt this way before, or that you lost the feeling a long time ago. I invite you to commit to being completely Honest. I'll tell you right now, it feels AMAZING.

If you're completely Honest with yourself, nothing, no one, and no circumstance will cause you to revert to old destructive habits. You will be liberated from all the chains that bind you. That's the honest truth.

Note: A word of caution. Honesty does not conflict with Imagination. Honesty doesn't mean that you focus on the negative, dwell on it, and beat yourself up for it. That's exactly what the Bully wants you to do.

Honesty is being willing to take responsibility for your actions and strive to improve your behaviors and beliefs.

Similarly, Imagination is not lying. When you Imagine, you are feeling, believing, and stating the truth. Sure, some of your declarations may not have yet come into existence, but they are essentially and fundamentally true. And by imagining them, you will make them not only true, but real.

I'd like to make you a promise:

If you are Honest with yourself, you will never relapse.

It's quite the bold statement, I know. I have been challenged innumerable times about what causes and prevents relapse. But I can assure you that every relapse begins with a lie. It's a lie told you by The Bully. It's a lie you tell yourself.

Honesty is the key to remaining happy, healthy, and sober. It's one of the most powerful concepts I teach because it both helps my clients be responsible for the choices they make and protects their loved ones from the harmful lies.

I repeat, if you are Honest with yourself, you will NEVER relapse.

WAS I HONEST WITH MYSELF TODAY?

When I was taking my first steps into sobriety, I had a mentor, life coach, and friend whom I met with every week for a year.

He helped me make extraordinary progress in overcoming my addictions and was always available when I needed support, but he had one condition for meeting me: I had to be completely honest with him. If I told a lie, our meetings were over.

It was extremely challenging for me. I had become accustomed to telling lies. I had hid my addiction from teachers, family members, and coaches for years. I had become a master of deception, addicted to lying the same way I was addicted to drugs.

But I disciplined myself and always told my mentor the truth anyway. I told him about my successes, the times I made it through the day without using. I told him about my shortcomings and relapses as well.

In this time, I discovered the power of Honesty. By being honest with my mentor, I was forced to be honest with myself as well. I had no more room for denial. I had to admit hard things to myself, but those hard things helped me face up to my problems and take control of my life.

This leads me to the second step of your nighttime reflection.

After you list three things you're grateful for, ask yourself this question: was I honest with myself today?

Really parse your day. Examine everything you said, every thought you had, and every time The Bully tried to get you down.

If you can say that you were Honest with yourself, then you are on the road to recovery. If the answer is no several nights in a row, you may be in relapse mode.

The good thing is, just from doing this exercise, you are already working towards total Honesty. Even if you weren't honest during the day, admitting that to yourself is in itself an act of Honesty. You will become more accustomed to telling yourself the truth, and when The Bully comes along, you'll be ready.

If you perform this evening ritual diligently, it will have the same effect as my mentor did on me. You will be accountable to someone (yourself) for your Honesty.

⬙ Assignment

Put a reminder in your phone to remind you at the end of every day to stand in front of the mirror and be accountable to yourself. Ask yourself the question, "Have I been honest with myself and others today?"

If the answer is yes, great job, you are in a safe place! Do it again tomorrow. If the answer is no, assess yourself and find out why. If you answer no for several days in a row, you are in relapse mode! Figure out how you can try again tomorrow and be successful with honesty.

Again, if you are honest with yourself you will never relapse.

> **If you master the first eleven steps of AA, but not the twelfth, you will drink again. If you master step twelve you'll never touch another drop.**

 Definition

JOY: Our natural state. Enlightenment.

 Overview

THE POWER OF SIMPLICITY

I would like you to read an excerpt from James Allen's book, *The Life Triumphant*, under the chapter "Simplicity and Freedom," which illustrates the way that I view Joy:

"What," asked the learned man of the Buddhist saint who had acquired a wide reputation for sanctity and wisdom – "what is the most fundamental thing in Buddhism?"

The saint replied, "The most fundamental thing in Buddhism is to cease from evil and learn to do good."

"I did not ask you," said the learned man, "to tell me what every child of three knows; I want you to tell me what is the most profound, the most subtle, the most important thing in Buddhism."

"The most profound, the most subtle, the most important thing in in Buddhism," said the saint, "is to cease from evil and learn to do well. It is true that a child of three my know it, but grey-haired old men fail to put it into practice."

The commentator goes on to say that the learned man did not want facts; he did not want Truth; he wanted to be given some subtle metaphysical speculation which would give rise to another speculation, and then to another and another, and so afford him an opportunity of bringing into play the wonderful intellect which he was so proud."

At the end of the day, it's all about Joy.

Why did you start reading this workbook? Why have you stayed on the train for this long? Probably because you want to experience more Joy in your life.

Joy is the ultimate goal. It's what all of this is for.

No matter your aspirations, faith, or disposition, I think we can all agree that creating and experiencing Joy is one of the main purposes of life.

This is why the last question I'd have you ask before you go to sleep is related to Joy. I've already talked about listing three things you're Grateful for and evaluating your Honesty. After all this I want you to ask yourself: Where did I experience Joy today?

Where did you choose to see the good and feel Gratitude? What made you smile? What made life worth living?

If your answer is "No, I did not feel Joy," then you have to ask yourself why. What things do you need to let go? What future events are causing you to worry? What behaviors do you need to change to allow yourself to enjoy life?

If you're not feeling Joy, you're not living up to your Personal Declaration Statement. Joy is all about having a purpose in life and striving to make that purpose part of your reality.

The truth is, you have the RIGHT to feel Joy. It's one of the few things in life you are entitled to. That's because Joy is life! It's time for you to start living. Choose to create Joy every day of your life.

Joy is our natural state

I want you to do a quick exercise right now as you are reading this. Take a moment and think back to the time when you were in elementary school. Remember recess? What was it like? Who were your friends? What games did you play?

Take a minute, close your eyes, and really take yourself back there.

I'm willing to bet money that you are smiling right now. Why? Because in most cases remembering our early childhood brings us Joy.

It was a simpler time. As children we were carefree, curious, and fascinated by everything life had to offer. We weren't afraid of the future even though we didn't know what it would hold. We experienced Joy all the time.

So what happened? What changed?

As we start growing older we tell ourselves a different a story. We learn to reason through trial and error. We learn lessons from our mistakes. We even think that we can use our experiences to predict the future.

The problem comes when our experience turns to irrationality. We use our cognitive abilities to construct the worst possible future for ourselves where the worst possible outcomes always occur. We then use these irrational constructions to feel nothing but worry, anxiety, and self-hatred.

We think we have outgrown the fantasy world that children inhabit, when in reality, Joy is our natural state.

When children fall down while playing and scrape their knee, sure, they cry for a bit. But in less than ten minutes they will have forgotten all about it and get right back to playing and enjoying life.

It's because children live in the moment. Our natural state of being is to feel the Joy of life, but as adults, we are always preoccupied with regretting the past and fearing the future. It's not that our circumstances have changed, it's just that we've forgotten how to see the good.

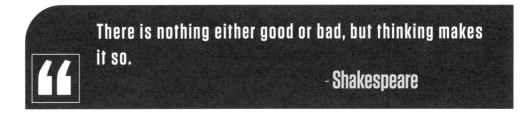

There is nothing either good or bad, but thinking makes it so.
                                                    - Shakespeare

If you choose to think the world is good, you can revert to your natural state of being and experience Joy all the time.

Joy is living in the moment

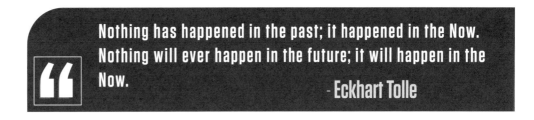

Nothing has happened in the past; it happened in the Now. Nothing will ever happen in the future; it will happen in the Now.
                                                    - Eckhart Tolle

Do you remember reading that quote? Yes, THAT one right there by Eckhart Tolle. You just barely read it, but already it's in the past. That's how quickly time moves.

The nature of linear time is such that we can remember past events and anticipate future ones, but really we can only exist in the present.

All we have is NOW. Every second, every moment, is NOW.

So what will you do with your Now? In terms of Joy you have only two choices: feel Joy, or don't.

What you can't do is choose to feel Joy in the future. You can't control future you. Only present you has the power to experience Joy and live life to the fullest. It's like the old adage goes: tomorrow never comes.

In a more practical sense, hoping to feel Joy in the future while remaining miserable today just doesn't work. I can tell you from experience.

During the years of my addiction, I was always hoping for some change in my circumstances, something that would come along and make it easier to break my habits. I procrastinated getting better, thinking I could handle just one more hit. "On Monday I'll start fresh," I told myself. "Next month for sure."

In the end, it took a little girl at a lemonade stand to help me realize I had been lying to myself. By seizing that moment and choosing to perform the small act of giving her my change, I finally felt it. I experienced Joy for the first time in years. That moment turned out to be an act of Greatness for me, and it's changed my life.

If you are future tripping, worrying about what's going to happen to you, or beating yourself up for past mistakes, STOP NOW!

Stop doing that! You can't change the past and you can't predict the future, so why are you letting them rule your life?

The reality is that life is a series of problems. If you are waiting for some trial to pass before feeling Joy, I assure you, another one will come along by the time this one ends.

So don't wait! You have the power to feel Joy in the present moment, so why not give it a try? I promise you, the future will work itself out.

Now I'm not, of course, suggesting that you forget about the future altogether. You need to have goals and planning is essential to success—just think about it in terms of the present. What will you do TODAY to help make your future aspirations come true? What Joy can you experience right away?

Similarly, reflection and memory can be powerful tools as long as they allow us to feel Joy, not regret. Like the exercise at the beginning of this article, it's good to remember and bring a piece of Joy felt long ago into our lives today. It's not good to feel sad that the circumstances of our lives have changed.

The song "Stressed Out" by Twenty One Pilots describes this error perfectly:

"Wish we could turn back time

To the good ol' days

When our momma sang us to sleep,

But now we're stressed out."

The truth is, you don't have to be stressed out. There is nothing inherent to adulthood demanding that we have to be miserable. Sure, we have more responsibility, but we also have more freedom. True Joy is rejoicing in our independence and learning to appreciate each stage of life.

Being stressed out is a choice. You can choose instead to live in the moment and experience joy in the same way that a child does. In a way, you CAN turn back time by taking the Joyful, carefree mindset you had as a child and bringing it into your present.

Tool

Joy is in the small things

Once, when I was directing a group recovery meeting, one of our clients rushed in about half an hour late. He had never been late for group before, so I politely asked him what held him up. He reported that he had started walking to arrive at the meeting on time, but on his way he had become captivated by an ant pile.

He observed the ants for half an hour as they busily went about constructing their colony. The ants didn't know he was there looming over them, but he noticed them and found it fascinating. It made him so happy to watch, it wasn't something he had done since he was a kid, but that day he felt compelled to do so.

When you slow down to really appreciate life in the moment, the simplest of things can bring you Joy. The world is so full of beauty that, no matter what your circumstances are, it is possible to experience Joy every single day.

Our ultimate goal in life should be to experience Joy the way we did when we were kids. That means we will have to make changes to our thoughts, behaviors, and most importantly, belief systems. If we can do this, however, there is NO reason that we can't feel Joy.

Whenever my clients are feeling anxiety, I tell them to ask themselves what they were thinking about. It starts with an irrational thought every single time. Joy, on the other hand, originates from living in the moment.

I should mention that many people have used the mantra "Live in the Moment" to actually encourage destructive behaviors. Carpe diem and YOLO abound.

Don't get confused.

When I say "live in the moment" I am not saying that you should go out and do something that's bad for you with no regard for the consequences. Doing things that scare you can be healthy. Doing things that are dangerous is not.

This is where your intuition comes into play. You will know the right things to do, what makes you feel joy and what brings you misery. Just make sure you're Honest with yourself. If you watch out for justifications and the lies of The Bully, you will never err.

Sometimes people ask me why I choose to use the word "Joy" instead of the word "happiness." I'll explain. While happiness is an emotion, fleeting, ethereal, Joy is a lifestyle. It's an immersive and fundamental mindset.

Sure, Joy often comes in little moments, strung out over a period of time, but by living constantly in the present, those moments will coalesce and form one Joyful whole. You will know you have made it when you can confidently say, as many of my clients now do, that you experience Joy constantly.

As I've said before, Joy is the goal of life, but by now you should realize that Joy is a journey, not a destination.

Joy is not an event. It's not something that happens to you. It something that you have to choose to create. As you learn to do so, you will find that it's not difficult. Joy is everywhere. All we have to do is take it in.

Assignment

Ask yourself if you experienced Joy today. Take some time to write down what Joy means to you and how you felt it throughout the day. If you did not, is something off? What can you do differently to experience Joy?

_____
_____
_____
_____
_____
_____
_____
_____
_____
_____
_____
_____
_____
_____
_____
_____
_____
_____
_____
_____
_____
_____
_____
_____
_____

CONCLUSION

Now that you have been through the program, the rest is up to you. The ball is in your court to put in the work and focus on the change within you. Once you have started working, the next step is to share it. When we help someone else, it empowers us. Ferdinand Foch said it best, "the most powerful weapon on earth is the human soul on fire." When we help others it lights our soul on fire!

Neale Donald Walsch said, "If you want to be...Give it away." I believe this to be one of, if not, the most powerful principle on the planet.

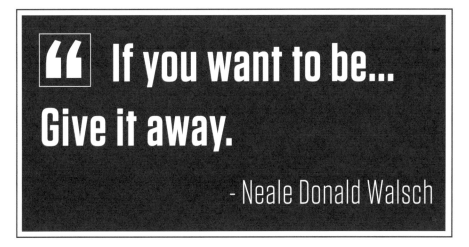

PRINCIPLES

Definition

PRINCIPLE: A principle is a law, something that is true and constant. like gravity.It serves as the foundation for a system of belief, behavior, or for a chain of reasoning. Never changes. It will work for you or against you but it is always there. 24/7.

Overview

Along with the 7 Principles of Daily Sobriety that you learned as part of this recoverED program, there are a number of other principles that are taught throughout this and other TSI programs. I wanted to compile and share them with you, as they are good snippets of ways to be mindful through your recovery journey. Some of these are simply quotes, some are activities. My hope is that they enrich your toolbox and keep them with you as you need them.

"The doer of true actions, who pursues sound methods grounded on right principles, will not need to strive and struggle for good results; they will be there as the effects of his righteous rule of life. He will reap the fruit of his own actions and the reaping will be in gladness and peace." *James Allen, Foundation Stones to Happiness and Success; Good Results*

THOUGHT CREATES THE EMOTION - EVERY TIME!

Negative emotions of fear, worry, anxiety, guilt, shame, depression, sadness all start with a thought.

Positive emotions of love, joy, happiness, compassion, sympathy, calm, peace, love, expansion of your light, all start with a thought. We think and then we feel.

THOUGHTS CREATE THINGS

Have everyone in the room look at everything in the room, the lights, floor, paint, light switches, chairs, the clothes they are wearing all started by a thought in someone's mind. I.e. Steve Jobs had the idea in his mind of the smartphone and now we all have one in our hands.

WHAT WE FOCUS ON INCREASES

Very simple to understand but with most people, this principle is working against them. If I am focusing on how hard something is, it will be and get more difficult. If I focus on the talk I have to give next week and how scary it will be, anxiety will increase and increase. If i focus on how great today is, gratitude will increase. Most people who are struggling is because they are focused on the wrong things.

WHERE ATTENTION GOES ENERGY FLOWS

James Allen said it best, "When mental energy allowed to follow the line of least resistance, and to fall into easy channels, it is called weakness. When it is gathered, focused, and forced into upward and different directions, it becomes power…"

BELIEF DICTATES BEHAVIOR

There is an old Latin proverb that states, "believe that you have it and you have it." If I believe I am a criminal, I will behave like a criminal. If I believe I am a good person, I will behave like a good person. Mark 11:24

IF YOU WANT TO BE… GIVE IT AWAY

If you want to be or possess anything, give it away. If I want to be happy, go make someone happy and you will BE happy. So simple but so, so powerful. You can't give away what you don't possess. You will realize when you give it away, you had it all along.

THERE IS NOTHING WRONG WITH YOU

This is the Greatest truth on the planet. "The most delightful surprise in life is to suddenly recognize that there is nothing wrong with you."

FAST IS SLOW - SLOW IS FAST

This has to do with building healthy relationships. If we try to quickly (fast) build or repair a failed relationship, the process for that coming to pass will be very, very slow, if at all. But, if you slowly massage the relationship, the process is very fast for it to become healthy again.

WHAT FOLLOWS I AM FOLLOWS YOU

If you say you are an addict or criminal, it will always follow you.

HONEST = CLEAN

If you're are honest with yourself you will never relapse.

ADDITIONAL
RESOURCES

HANDOUTS

For the following handouts, please send an email to todd@toddsylvesterinspires.com

- The Worst Bully You'll Ever Encounter
- The Power of Intent
- The 3 Core Beliefs
- The Buck Stops Here
- Standing Alone
- Are You Kidding Me
- Stop Acting Like You're Not Amazing
- Personal Declaration
- Letter of Greatness
- Embrace the Silence
- Mindfulness, Count to 123
- The 10-minute Miracle
- Date Night with Your Kids
- 100% Responsible
- The Hardest Chemical to Come Off
- 400 Challenge

- *Man's Search for Meaning*- Viktor Frankl

- *As a Man Thinketh*- James Allen

- *True Love*- Thich Nhat Hanh

- *The Power of Now*- Eckhart Tolle

- *The Truth About Addiction and Recovery*- Stanton Peele

- *Psyco-Cyberntics*- Maxwell Maltz

- *Think and Grow Rich*- Napoleon Hill

- *The Psychology of Winning*- Denis Waitley

- *The Alchemist*- Paulo Coelho

- *A New Earth, Awakening to Your Life's Purpose*- Eckhart Tolle

- *Find Your Why*- Simon Sinek

- *The Purpose Driven Life*- Rick Warren

- *Mind is the Master*- James Allen

- *It's Time to Start Living*- Todd Sylvester

Literacy is a bridge from misery to hope.

- Kofi Annan

DEFINITIONS

ADDICTION:	The perpetual avoidance of legitimate suffering
ANXIETY:	A misuse of your imagination
ABUSE:	The fuel that will eventually make you tough as hell
BORED:	Not comfortable in my own skin. Need a distraction to be okay.
CLEAN:	I am done
CRAVING:	An opportunity
DECISION:	A purposeful commitment to make up your mind to do (or not do) something.
DECLARE:	To make known as a determination. Acknowledging that you already possess something.
DEPRESSION:	Pretending to be someone you're not / Past
DISEASE:	Victim Stance / Excuse / Trap
ENLIGHTENMENT:	The end of Suffering – Buddha
GREATNESS:	Greatness is refusing the drugs or alcohol when no one is around. Greatness is doing the right thing.
GRATITUDE:	The quality of being thankful. The most powerful stimulant on the planet.
HONESTY:	The foundation of never relapsing
IMAGINE:	To form a mental image of something not present
JOY:	Our natural state. Enlightenment.
FUTURE:	Time regarded as still to come
FUTURE TRIPPING:	Worrying about the future, not living in the present
HARD:	Uncomfortable
INTENT:	An anticipated outcome that is intended or that guides your planned actions
LAW OF ATTRACTION:	The attractive, magnetic power of the Universe that draws similar energies together.
LOVE OF SELF:	The instinct by which one's actions are directed to the promotion of one's own welfare or well-being.
PAST:	Gone by in time and no longer existing
PRESENT/NOW:	Existing or occurring now
A SMILE:	Realization
SOBRIETY:	The periods between using
TOO HARD:	Victim stance / Telling ourselves we can't do it
TRIGGER:	Opportunity
SELF-PITY:	The worst disease on the planet

Made in United States
Troutdale, OR
05/16/2025

31396153R00052